TH
Sunday
COOKBOOK

Gretel Beer is cookery columnist of the *Sunday Express*. Among the numerous other newspapers and journals to which she has contributed articles on food and travel are *Vogue*, the *Daily Telegraph*, *House and Garden*, the *Sunday Times*, the *Scotsman* and many women's magazines. Her previous books are *Austrian Cooking*, *The Diabetic Gourmet*, *Ice Cream Dishes* and *Sandwiches for Parties and Picnics*.

THE
Sunday Express
COOKBOOK

GRETEL BEER

Fontana/Collins

First published by Fontana Paperbacks 1986

Set in 11 on 12½ Linotron Garamond
Made and printed in Great Britain by
William Collins Sons & Co. Ltd, Glasgow

To
Max Davidson
and
James Kinlay

Contents

Introduction

Writing a cookery column for the *Sunday Express* is exactly like preparing food for one's family and friends. Will they like the new dish I have discovered? The 'classic' I have adjusted and the 'special' given to me by a favourite chef? Will the flavouring be too strong – too mild – too exotic? Will they like what I am cooking – or advocate that they should cook?

That is why I positively thrive on readers letters. 'And always remember', said a wily old bird, 'that they will only write to complain, never to compliment.' Actually, he was wrong. Readers do write to compliment and that's when I all but purr with pleasure. 'We followed your recipe for cooking the Christmas goose implicitly and it was superb.' That made my Christmas for many years to come. And the letter which simply said, 'I feel I must send you a line to say how very much I have appreciated your recipes – the only complaint I can make is that the waistline suffers – but who cares in the face of such delicious food. With thanks from my family and myself.' Sounds as sweet as the violins of the Vienna Philharmonic . . .

Not that all readers' letters are like that. The very first letter I received after my first column had appeared in the *Sunday Express* was short and to the point: 'I have today made your cherry slices and the birds in my garden are now tucking into them. Shall not buy the *Sunday Express* for a few weeks to make up the cost of what I have just lost.' I expected to be fired after that – but all I got was an indulgent 'Well, tastes do differ' after the whole office had tucked into the self-same cherry cake.

9

The second letter was puzzling rather than admonishing – a long tirade against a very simple dish of potatoes cooked in a creamy sauce flavoured with marjoram, and a perfect accompaniment to cold meat.

At least so I thought, but: 'I question why any "newspaper cook" should take a devilish delight in thinking up recipes for the unwary.' Actually, it was not a newspaper cook but my grandmother who had thought up that particular recipe and it certainly was not for the unwary – so I took the rather unprecedented step of telephoning the number given at the top of the letter (a rather grand address, incidentally).

'I really must apologize,' said the voice at the other end. 'After I wrote that letter I found that the recipe was quite delicious.'

'Oh?'

'Well, I let it get cold and it was delicious, absolutely delicious.'

'Oh? But it was a hot accompaniment to cold meat!'

'Never mind that. It made a delicious sandwich filling.'

'Are you sure we are talking about the same dish?'

My recipe was read out to me.

'Such a delicious filling for sandwiches. Like pâté.'

There is no answer to that . . .

I love readers' indulgence, though. Like when a small 'printing devil' turned '1½ lb potatoes' into '1½ potatoes' and I got letters asking, 'What size potatoes?' Or worse still – telescoped the amounts of sugar and gelatine in one particular recipe, ending up with 3½ oz gelatine – enough to set a whole party rigid – and on the Royal Wedding Day too! I got a whole lot of rather comforting letters, saying, 'It could not possibly have been your fault' – and one which sternly admonished me with, 'Never let it happen again.'

Sometimes I get lovely requests – like a heartfelt cry for the special chocolate cake a reader had enjoyed many years ago – 'and the cook's name was Marie' – and the request for the special almond pastries enjoyed as a student in the 'gods' of the Vienna Opera House before the war. Surprisingly I could oblige – with the help of my favourite cookery writer in Austria.

There was also the time I was called to the telephone while on holiday on an island thousands of miles away from home. I padded to the telephone, blinded by the sun and spreading soft sand all over the restaurant floor. The voice from home came over faintly, but it had a ring of authority: 'A reader wants to know,' it said, 'if you double the quantity for the chocolate cake, how long has it got to stay in the oven?' I shook the sand out of my sandals and the water out of my ears. 'Which chocolate cake?' It appeared it was one which had been published several years ago. Waiters with loaded trays flashed past me as I tried to give a sensible answer – and I did, eventually. 'Just tell me,' I said to the voice coming over from halfway across the world, 'could this not have waited until I got back?'

'Sorry to have bothered you,' said the voice, 'but the reader said it's urgent. The cake is in the oven right now.'

My favourite letters from readers, though, are those that say that my recipes have become 'so dog-eared as to be illegible' or – better still and as was the case not so long ago – that 'the dog has chewed them up' – and could there not be a collection of them . . . ? This is why I have written this book – a collection of some of the recipes published in the *Sunday Express* plus quite a few as yet unpublished ones which the dog has not yet had a chance of getting into his paws.

Gretel Beer

Some explanations
Preferences, prejudices and other useful things

MUSHROOMS

Dried boletus mushrooms are an absolute joy – albeit an expensive one – when used in cooking. Depending on their country of origin they are sold as Cepes or Porcini or Steinpilze, but watch out for the small print which sometimes says 'boletus and other mushrooms'. Nothing wrong with that and they may even be cheaper, but the packet will contain other and possibly lesser flavoured mushrooms as well as boletus. Dried mushrooms often contain quite a bit of sand and it is always safer to soak them first. Do not waste the liquid in which they were soaked though – simply strain it through a sieve which has been lined with kitchen paper to trap the sand and add the liquid to whatever dish you are cooking with the mushrooms.

VANILLA SUGAR

Some of the vanilla sugar sold in packets contains artificial flavouring. If you want to be sure of the true flavour of vanilla, keep a vanilla pod in a jar of sugar and use the sugar whenever a recipe calls for 'vanilla sugar'.

TOMATOES

After the small round tomatoes which seem to be getting rounder and harder all the time and taste of absolutely nothing (though perfect, I am told, for cutting into perfect quarters for a salad – if you want quartered tasteless tomatoes in your salad, that is), we now have so-called 'beef tomatoes' which are large and round and taste of absolutely nothing. If you want tomatoes which taste of tomato – warmed by the sun and full of flavour – look out for the nice gnarly ones – or grow them yourself, which is not as difficult as it may sound.

PEPPER

There is black pepper and white pepper and green pepper and pink pepper – the last one hailed as the great new culinary discovery and now declared as possibly dangerous to health, though that is probably overstating it as well. I do not believe in 'freshly milled black pepper' with practically everything – particularly not in light delicate sauces and snowy white mashed potatoes where it looks as if ashes had been scattered like confetti. White pepper is a perfectly good spice with its proper place in some recipes, where it is preferable to black pepper – and it should be used as such. And as to the 'freshly milled' – of course pepper, whether black or white, is best when freshly ground, but there are more culinary sins committed every hour of the day than using ground black or white pepper if you are in a hurry.

ASPIC JELLY

Unless you make your own – which is not difficult but time-consuming – use a good brand of savoury aspic crystals. I like the Swiss brand of Haco – a personal preference, I admit – and to enhance it further I infuse a few lovage leaves to give a better flavour, plus occasionally a dash of wine or wine vinegar, depending on the dish.

BREADCRUMBS

I distrust most shop-bought breadcrumbs. They are either of the nasty, yellow-dyed kind at which any respectable goldfish would turn up its nose or they look like sweepings from the bakery floor). Far better to make your own.

GARLIC
A trick culled from my favourite chef: take a small or large screw-top jar and half fill it with crushed garlic cloves. Top up with olive oil and keep in a cool and dark place. Shake or stir gently from time to time. Marvellous for salads and other dishes where you do not want crushed garlic bits to float around. Top up with oil whenever you use some and stir gently.

FLOUR
Except for very rare occasions I always use plain flour. Some recipes call for 'strong' flour and this has been indicated.

CREAM
All cream used in my recipes is double cream unless otherwise stated.

BUTTER
I use only unsalted butter. You can always add salt when required, but you can't take it away once it has been added.

QUANTITIES
Appetites vary and so do portions, but generally speaking most recipes are intended for 4–6 people unless otherwise stated.

Soups

I think I could live quite happily on soup alone. For a long time, anyhow. Rich and hearty soups which are practically a meal in themselves, and light and delicate ones – so light and delicate that a second helping is always called for – after which I'd probably want only a little cheese and some fruit.

Some of my soups rely for their flavour entirely on the basic ingredients which go into the making – herbs and delicate wood mushrooms, for instance, or the smooth blend of butter and milk, Brussels sprouts and bacon as for *potage Brabançon* – but for others the choice of stock is all important. Ham stock has a natural affinity with pulses and if you cook a ham or a piece of gammon or one of the nice smoked loins of pork now so widely available, save the liquid. Let it get quite cold and then skim off all the fat – and there is usually quite a bit of fat – and then use the stock for soup.

And for the recipes which call for chicken or beef stock – or just 'good stock'? If you have been able to make your own stock – from a chicken carcass, or marrow or veal bones – this is splendid, of course, but failing that there is absolutely nothing wrong with a good stock cube. In fact it is infinitely preferable to the liquid emanating from a stockpot which has been kept simmering for days and to which bits of this and that have been added without discrimination.

I have been experimenting lately with an imported chicken concentrate sold in tins which I find preferable to stock cubes, though it is expensive and has to be kept in the fridge. It is excellent and I understand that there is also a beef equivalent, though I have not yet been able to track it down.

Anchovy soup

A lovely old recipe dating back to the Vienna Congress – the one that did not sit but danced. You will be able to discern the flavour of anchovies from the finished product merely as a hint of something rather delicious but undefinable.

1 heaped tablespoon butter
1 flat tablespoon flour
2 heaped tablespoons chopped parsley or parsley root
2 heaped tablespoons grated celeriac
4 fl oz (100ml) dry white wine

1½ pints (850ml) good beef or chicken stock
6–8 anchovy fillets
1 tablespoon chopped parsley
4 fl oz (100ml) cream
salt and pepper
fried croûtons

Melt the butter in a saucepan. Add the flour, stir, then add the parsley (or parsley root) and the grated celeriac. Stir, then pour in the white wine and stir again. Add the stock and simmer gently for 20–30 minutes. Finely scrape the anchovy fillets, add the tablespoon chopped parsley and the cream. Add this to the soup and reheat very gently. Season with pepper and very little salt. Serve with croûtons fried in butter.

Austrian Christmas soup

There are probably as many versions of this traditional soup as there are varieties of fish in the Danube, some using soft roes only, others insisting that only hard roe will give the right consistency. Some recipes call for a very smooth mixture while others provide a soup which has a good bit of 'bite' to it.

Either way, it is practically a meal in itself. My own version includes small pieces of hard roe, giving a pleasant contrast of texture. In Austria fresh river fish is used for this soup – mostly heads and tails plus all the trimmings and of course the roes, but the soup is still excellent if made with a mixture of any well-flavoured white fish and roes – and herring roes are particularly good for this.

fish trimmings, including a few heads if possible
salt
a few peppercorns
1–2 bay leaves
sprig each of thyme, rosemary and marjoram
a few lovage leaves
a few twists of lemon rind
a few mushroom stalks (or dried mushrooms)
dash of wine vinegar
1 heaped tablespoon butter
2 carrots
1 medium-sized onion

1 small celeriac
1–2 tomatoes
a few slivers of red or green pepper
1 lb (450g) firm-fleshed white fish (see above)
1 lb (450g) fresh roes, preferably a mixture of soft and hard
1 tablespoon flour
¼ pint (140ml) red wine
a good pinch of sugar
¼ pint (140ml) sour cream
fried croûtons

Put the fish trimmings, salt, peppercorns, the herbs, lemon rind and mushroom stalks (or dried mushrooms) into a large saucepan. Cover with 3 pints of water, add a good dash wine vinegar and leave to simmer gently for about 1 hour.

While this is happening, melt the butter in a saucepan and grate into it the carrots, the onion and the celeriac. Add the tomatoes and the pepper strips. Cover and leave to simmer until the vegetables are soft.

Poach the fish and the roes in the fish stock (it is best to tie the roes in a muslin bag first). Lift out and keep them separate.

When the vegetables are tender, dust them with flour, stir,

17

and add the wine, a pinch of sugar and about a ladleful of strained fish stock. Leave to simmer. Lift the fish from the stock and flake it into the vegetables; also add the mushroom stalks or dried mushrooms. There is usually quite a bit of good flesh on a fish head – scrape it out and add it as well. I know it sounds tedious, but real connoisseurs will tell you that the best flesh on a carp, for instance, is on the head. Strain the fish stock over the fish and the vegetables. Add half the cooked roes – if you have used a mixture of hard and soft roes, add the soft roes only. Leave to simmer for another 5 or 10 minutes, then put everything through a blender or a coarse sieve. Do not use a fine sieve – it would make the mixture too smooth. Chop the remaining roes into cubes and add. Stir in the sour cream and reheat gently. Adjust the seasoning if necessary – the soup should have a definite 'sharp' tang. Serve with plenty of hot buttery croûtons.

Potage Brabançon

1 oz (25g) butter	18 oz (500g) Brussels sprouts
4 oz (110g) lean bacon, diced	about 11 fl oz (300ml) boiling milk
1 medium-sized onion, chopped	salt and pepper
a few celery tops or ½ small celeriac, chopped	grated nutmeg
18 oz (500g) peeled and diced potatoes	2 egg yolks
	4 tablespoons cream

Melt the butter in a large saucepan, add the diced bacon and cook gently until the fat begins to run. Add the chopped onion and celery (or celeriac) and cook over low heat until they colour slightly, then add the diced potatoes and the cleaned

Brussels sprouts. Pour in 1¾ pints (1 litre) water and simmer gently until the potatoes are soft. Purée the mixture or use a blender or food processor. Thin the soup with boiling milk to the required consistency, then season with salt, pepper and a grating of nutmeg.

Whisk together the egg yolks and the cream in a warmed soup terrine, pour in the soup, whisking constantly, and serve at once.

Finely chopped cooked chestnuts make a splendid garnish for festive occasions.

Mushroom soup

8 oz (225g) mushrooms – wood mushrooms for preference
1 small onion
2 oz (50g) butter
1 tablespoon chopped parsley
1 teaspoon chopped fresh marjoram

1 scant tablespoon flour
2¼ pints (1.25 litres) good stock
salt and pepper
1 bay leaf
4–5 tablespoons cream or sour cream

Thinly slice the mushrooms. Peel and chop the onion. Melt the butter in a large saucepan, add the chopped onion and allow it to soften over low heat. Add the mushrooms, parsley and marjoram. Cover and cook very gently for about 8 minutes. Dust with flour, stir and then gradually add the stock. Also add salt, pepper and the bay leaf and simmer for about 20 minutes. Remove the bay leaf. Blend the cream with a little of the hot soup, then stir it into the remaining soup. Reheat gently, adjust seasoning if necessary and serve with fried croûtons or with

19

crispy bits of bacon – or both. Do not sprinkle them over the soup, but serve separately.

Creamy mushroom and potato soup

½ oz (15g) dried boletus mushrooms
2 heaped tablespoons butter
1 medium-sized onion, chopped
3–4 oz (85–110g) white parts of a leek, chopped
5–6 oz (140–160g) potatoes, peeled and sliced
1½ pints (800ml) chicken or veal stock

1 tablespoon finely chopped fresh marjoram
salt and white pepper
a little grated nutmeg or mace
6 fl oz (170ml) cream or sour cream
1 heaped tablespoon finely chopped fresh chervil

Put the dried mushrooms into a sieve and rinse them under a warm tap, then tip them into a cup and cover with warm water. Leave to stand until the mushrooms have softened slightly.

Melt 1 tablespoon of the butter in a saucepan, add the onion and the leek and soften over a low flame. Add the potatoes, stir and then pour on the stock. Leave to simmer until the potatoes are cooked.

In a separate pan, melt the remaining butter. Take the softened mushrooms out of the liquid and add. Brown the mushrooms very lightly, then carefully strain in the liquid in which they were soaked (there is usually a residue of fine sand, hence all that straining and soaking). Add the marjoram and simmer gently until the mushrooms are soft.

Purée the potatoes and the leek and return them to the liquid in which they were cooked. Add the mushrooms and their liquid and leave to simmer for another 5 minutes. Season with salt, white pepper and a sprinkling of nutmeg or mace. Stir in the cream or sour cream and reheat very gently. Serve sprinkled with finely chopped chervil.

Creamy potato soup

6 large potatoes
1 medium-sized onion
1 clove garlic
salt
1 heaped tablespoon butter
1 carrot, sliced
1 small celeriac, sliced (or a few celery tops)
1 tomato

1 flat tablespoon chopped parsley
1 flat dessertspoon chopped marjoram
2½ pints (1.4 litres) ham stock
5 fl oz (140ml) sour cream
a little paprika

Peel and dice the potatoes. Peel and thinly slice the onion. Crush the garlic under the blade of a knife with a little salt. Heat the butter in a saucepan, add the onion and the garlic and simmer gently until softened and just tinged with colour. Add the potatoes, the sliced carrot and celeriac. Also add a roughly chopped tomato and the chopped herbs. Cover with the ham stock and simmer until the potatoes are soft, then push everything through a sieve. Reheat gently and adjust the seasoning if necessary. Either stir in the sour cream just before serving or put a large dollop of it to float on top of each soup bowl. Sprinkle with paprika.

Fried croûtons and grated cheese go well with this soup, or pour it into a large ovenproof bowl – or small individual soup bowls – and sprinkle with fried croûtons and grated cheese. Put the soup bowl into a hot oven or, in the case of individual soup bowls, under a hot grill, until the cheese has melted and browned a little.

Onion soup

4–6 medium-sized onions
2 heaped tablespoons butter
1 flat tablespoon flour
1½ pints (800ml) good clear
  stock
¼ pint (110ml) white wine

salt and pepper
grated nutmeg
4 thin slices bread
butter for frying
grated cheese

Peel the onions and cut them into very thin slices, the thinner the better. If you own a food processor this of course takes a matter of minutes, but if you have to cut them by hand (a mandoline cutter is splendid for the job too) do not skimp on this part of the job.

Melt the butter in a thick, large saucepan, then throw in the onions and leave to simmer very, very gently until the onions are soft, but not browned. It will take at least 20 minutes and this is the part which cannot be hurried – just be patient and shake the saucepan from time to time. When the onions are soft, turn up the heat, stir and allow the onions to colour a little – they should be a good golden colour – then dust with flour, stir again and let the flour take a little colour too. Now pour in the stock and the wine and season with salt, pepper and a little grated nutmeg. Leave to simmer for about 25 minutes.

Meanwhile cut the bread into quarters and fry gently in butter until golden brown on both sides. Put the bread into a soup bowl – or divide between individual bowls – and sprinkle grated cheese between the slices. Pour the boiling soup on to the fried bread slices, which will rise to the surface, and sprinkle a little more grated cheese over the top. Put into a very hot oven to brown, or, if using individual soup bowls, simply slip them under a hot grill for a few minutes. Serve at once.

Poacher's soup

3 medium-sized onions
2 leeks
½ small celery
½ lb (225g) mushrooms or ½ oz (15g) dried mushrooms
3 good tablespoons butter
1 tablespoon chopped parsley

1 tablespoon chopped lovage
1 bay leaf
pinch powdered cloves
salt and pepper
1 lightly heaped tablespoon potato flour
2–3 egg yolks
fried croûtons

Chop the onions finely. Clean the leeks, then cut them into thin rings. Chop the celery. Clean and slice the mushrooms. (If using dried mushrooms, soak them in a little warm water for about half an hour.) Melt the butter, add the chopped onions and simmer them gently until they are transparent. Add the sliced leeks, chopped celery and the sliced mushrooms. (If using dried mushrooms, add them as well, but keep the water in which they were soaked.) Stir the mixture until everything is well coated with butter, then add the chopped parsley and lovage, bay leaf, cloves and the seasonings. Stir again, then add about 2½ pints (1.4 litres) water. If you have used dried mushrooms, strain in the water in which they were soaked as well. Simmer until the vegetables are tender.

Slake the potato flour with just enough cold water to make a smooth paste, then whisk in the egg yolks. Gradually add to the hot soup and let it simmer gently until thickened – do not allow to come to the boil. Serve with plenty of croûtons fried crisply in butter.

Alternatively – and for a slightly more substantial dish – fry 6–8 small slices of bread in butter until golden brown on both sides. Line an ovenproof soup terrine (or use individual ovenproof dishes). Pour the hot soup over the bread which will rise to the top. Sprinkle thickly with grated Parmesan cheese and put under the grill or in a hot oven until browned on top.

Sorrel soup

2 large handfuls sorrel leaves (approx. 4 oz/110g)
2 heaped tablespoons butter
1 pint (575ml) good clear stock
2 teaspoons potato flour
2 egg yolks
4 tablespoons cream
salt and pepper

Wash the sorrel leaves and shake off any surplus water. Melt the butter, add the sorrel and simmer very gently until the leaves have 'collapsed'. Add the stock and simmer for another 10 minutes. Sieve or use a liquidiser. Slake the potato flour with a little of the liquid and add to the soup. Simmer gently for a few minutes – until well blended.

Whisk the egg yolks with the cream and pour into the hot soup. Reheat gently without letting it come to the boil. Season to taste.

Fried croûtons are a good accompaniment, but better still, float a little extra cream on top of each helping and serve with finely chopped hardboiled egg.

Tomato soup

2 lb (900g) tomatoes
2 tablespoons butter
salt and pepper
1 scant tablespoon sugar
small bunch of fresh basil

chicken stock – if necessary
5 fl oz (140ml) cream
chopped chives or parsley
fried croûtons

Wash the tomatoes, do not skin them, but just break them up roughly. Melt the butter in a large pan, add the tomatoes, salt, pepper, sugar and a small bunch of fresh basil. Cook very gently until the tomatoes are just beginning to disintegrate. Sieve the soup – or run it through the liquidizer and then sieve it – and, if necessary, thin it down with a little chicken stock. Reheat, stir in the cream and serve sprinkled with chopped chives or parsley and fried croûtons.

Soup made from pea pods

1 large saucepanful of pea pods
1 heaped tablespoon butter
6 spring onions

a handful of lettuce leaves
stock
5 fl oz (140ml) cream
salt and pepper

This soup is absolutely delicious, but it works only if you use really fresh pea pods – and use them as soon as you have shelled the peas. If you have a food processor or blender, just rinse the pods well under cold water and put them into a large saucepan, together with the butter, spring onions and lettuce leaves. Cover with a lid and simmer gently until the pods have softened, shaking the pan lightly from time to time. Cover with stock – liquid in which a ham bone has been cooked is ideal – and cook gently until the pods are tender. Put them through the blender or food processor and then sieve the resulting purée. Return the purée to the liquid, add the cream and seasoning and reheat gently.

If you do not have a blender or food processor, string the pea pods as you would French beans and at the same time bend each side of the pod in half; the thick inner skin will then peel off quite easily. This sounds – and is – a somewhat lengthy job, but rather pleasant to do, particularly when done sitting in the garden. From then onwards proceed as above, cooking the pods first in butter, then adding the stock and finally sieving them.

Fried croûtons go well with this soup and it tastes equally good served chilled with a sprinkling of chopped chives. Make sure that all trace of fat has been removed from the stock if serving the soup cold.

Rich winter soup

2 rashers bacon
1 large onion
1 large tablespoon butter
2–3 diced carrots
1 small diced celeriac (or quarter of a large one)
3–4 peeled and diced potatoes
3 oz (80g) sliced mushrooms
1 leek (green part only), sliced
1 tablespoon flour
2½ pints (1.4 litres) good stock
chopped parsley and marjoram
salt and pepper

Cut the bacon into small dice. Chop the onion finely. Heat the butter in a thick saucepan, add the diced bacon and the onion and simmer over low heat until the bacon is transparent and the onion has softened a little. Turn up the heat and allow the bacon and onion to brown lightly. Add the carrots, celeriac and potatoes. Stir so that everything is well mixed and then add the mushrooms and the sliced leek. Stir, then sprinkle with the flour and stir over heat until everything is lightly browned. Pour in the stock, add the parsley, marjoram and seasoning. Leave to simmer until the vegetables are tender. It tastes marvellous just as it is, but sometimes I put a small spoonful of cream into each soup bowl before pouring on the hot soup, or I hand a little grated cheese separately.

Creamy winter soup

1 large onion
2 tablespoons butter
1 clove garlic
18 oz (500g) potatoes
1 tablespoon finely chopped parsley
a little chopped marjoram and thyme
1 teaspoon caraway seeds
18 fl oz (500ml) water
18 fl oz (500ml) milk
salt
5 fl oz (140ml) cream
pinch of grated nutmeg
chopped chives

Chop the onion finely and simmer in the melted butter, together with the crushed clove of garlic, until transparent. Peel and cube the potatoes and add these to the onion and garlic, together with the parsley, herbs and caraway seeds. Stir, then pour in the water and the milk. Add a little salt and simmer gently over a low flame until the potatoes are just cooked – about 20 minutes. Pour the cream into a warmed soup terrine, add the nutmeg and then pour on the soup without stirring, so that there will be little soft clouds of cream floating on top. Sprinkle with chopped chives and serve.

27

Chervil soup

1¾ pints (1 litre) good beef
  stock
1 tablespoon flour
4 fl oz (110ml) cold milk
5 fl oz (140ml) cream

2 egg yolks
salt and white pepper
a good handful finely
  chopped chervil

Heat the stock. Mix the flour to a smooth paste with the cold milk and add to the hot stock. Simmer gently for 10 minutes.

Mix together cream and egg yolks. Pour the hot soup gradually on to the egg yolks and cream, whisking constantly. Return the mixture to the stove and whisk over low heat while the soup is reheating. Season with salt and white pepper. Stir in the chopped chervil and serve.

Herb soup

3 oz (90g) finely chopped
  fresh herbs, preferably a
  mixture of parsley, French
  marjoram, lovage, basil and
  very little thyme
2 tablespoons butter
3 tablespoons finely chopped
  onion

3 tablespoons butter
2 tablespoons flour
2 pints (1.1 litres) good stock
salt and pepper
1 tablespoon lemon juice
5 fl oz (140ml) sour cream

The herbs may of course be varied, but use only the smallest quantity of thyme since it tends to be overpowering. On occasion I have also added a little sorrel and some young spinach leaves.

Chop the herbs finely. Heat the 2 tablespoons of butter in a saucepan, add the chopped onion and allow it to soften in the butter. Add the chopped herbs and leave to simmer, gently shaking the pan from time to time.

In a separate saucepan melt the 3 tablespoons of butter and stir in the flour to make a blonde roux. Gradually, add the stock and the herbs. Simmer until well blended, then season with salt, pepper and the lemon juice. Just before serving, stir in the sour cream and reheat gently. Fried croûtons go well with this.

Hungarian cabbage soup
(serves 6–8 Hungarians)

This soup is called Korhelyleves in Hungary, where it is considered one of the best cures for anything from a broken heart to a broken leg. Essence of Tokay is said to grant eternal life – but since it is almost impossible to obtain and expensive beyond belief, Korhelyleves ranks a good second best!

2¼ lb (1kg) smoked pork rib
1–2 cloves garlic
3 medium-sized onions
2¼ lb (1kg) Sauerkraut
salt
1 tablespoon chopped dill
about 3¼ pints (2 litres) water

4 oz (110g) bacon
1 tablespoon flour
9 oz (250g) Hungarian
   sausages (see below)
½ pint (300ml) sour cream
1 dessertspoon paprika

Rinse the smoked pork under cold running water and dry with a kitchen towel. Peel and crush the garlic. Peel and chop the onions. Put the Sauerkraut into a large pan, add the pork, onions, garlic, salt and dill. Add plenty of water – about 3¼ pints – and simmer gently until the pork is tender – about 1½ hours. Take out the pork and cut into cubes. Dice the bacon and put the fat pieces into a frying pan first. Simmer until the fat begins to run, then add the lean pieces. Fry until golden brown and slightly crisp. Lift out with a slotted spoon and drain on kitchen paper. Stir the flour into the bacon fat and brown. Add the flour to the Sauerkraut, stir in the bacon, the pork and the sausage cut into slices. Stir in the sour cream and the paprika and simmer gently for 5 minutes. Adjust seasoning and serve.

In Hungary Debrecen sausages are used for this recipe. They are made of fairly coarsely chopped meat and are about the same size and shape as Frankfurter sausages. In fact they could be considered as 'farmhouse cousins' of Frankfurters, which can of course be used for this dish.

Instant spring soup

1 packet (10 oz/300g) deep-frozen French spring vegetables	1½ pints (850ml) good stock
	salt and pepper
	1 flat tablespoon butter
1 heaped tablespoon butter	chopped fresh herbs
1 scant tablespoon flour	

The deep-frozen vegetables I use for this particular recipe are packed by Bonduelle and contain small sprigs of young cauliflower, leeks, young carrots and small beans as well as diced celeriac – the last not strictly a spring vegetable, but it gives a rather special flavour to this soup.

Do not bother to defrost the vegetables. Melt the butter in a large saucepan and add the vegetables. Toss them in the melted butter, cover with a lid and allow them to simmer gently for about 10 minutes. Dust with flour and stir, letting the flour brown a little. Add the stock and simmer until the vegetables are just tender – no more. Adjust the seasoning, stir in the butter and serve with a sprinkling of fresh herbs.

Iced cucumber soup

2 large cucumbers
1 heaped tablespoon butter
a small bunch of fresh dill
salt and pepper
1¾ pints (1 litre) good stock,
   chicken for preference

5 fl oz (140ml) cream
a little extra cream for
   serving

Whether or not you peel the cucumber is a matter of taste – leaving it unpeeled produces a deeper colour. Sometimes I just run a potato peeler down the full length of the cucumber at about half-inch intervals.

Cut the cucumbers into thick slices. Melt the butter in a saucepan and add the cucumber, a few sprigs of dill (if there is no fresh dill, use freeze-dried), a pinch of salt and a little pepper. Cover with a lid and leave to simmer until the cucumber starts to look transparent. Add the stock and cook gently until the cucumber is soft. Add a few more sprigs of dill then put the mixture through the blender or food processor or rub it through a sieve. Stir in the cream and set to chill. Serve with a little more cream floating on top and decorate with a sprig of dill.

Iced tomato soup

1 tablespoon butter or olive
  oil
1 large onion, chopped
1½ lb (675g) very ripe
  tomatoes
1 bay leaf
a few peppercorns
a few fresh basil leaves
parsley and parsley root

a sprig of rosemary
salt
a good pinch sugar
dash of red wine
1 green pepper
5 fl oz (140ml) sour cream
cream or sour cream for
  serving
chopped chives for serving

Heat the butter or the olive oil in a large saucepan and soften
the chopped onion in this. Add the tomatoes, halved or
quartered or simply broken up. Do not bother to skin them –
in fact the skin will add a good bit of flavour. Also add the
herbs and seasonings and a good dash of red wine. Deseed the
green pepper and add that as well, reserving a small amount
for garnish. Leave to simmer gently until the tomatoes are
cooked, then push everything through a sieve. If necessary,
thin down a little with good clear stock, but usually the
tomatoes contain enough liquid. Taste and adjust seasoning,
adding a little more sugar and possibly a dash of wine vinegar
or lemon juice to give a distinctly piquant flavouring. Stir in
the sour cream and set to chill. Serve with a little cream or
sour cream floating on top and sprinkled with a small quantity
of finely chopped green pepper and some chopped chives.

Cream of lentil soup

½ lb (225g) brown lentils
2 pints (1.1 litres) ham stock
3 medium or large potatoes, peeled and cubed
small piece of celeriac or celery tops
1 carrot, chopped
1 bay leaf
sprig of thyme

a little thinly cut lemon peel
2 tablespoons butter
1 large onion, chopped
1 scant tablespoon flour
pepper
a little lemon juice
2 egg yolks
4 fl oz (110ml) single cream

Soak the lentils in cold water overnight or at least for 2 hours. Drain off the water. Put the lentils in a large saucepan, add the ham stock, potatoes, celeriac (or celery tops), carrot, bay leaf, thyme and lemon peel. Bring to the boil, then simmer gently until the lentils are soft. Melt the butter in a pan, add the chopped onion and allow to soften gently in the butter. Dust with the flour, brown lightly and add to the lentils, taking up all the scrapings from the pan. Leave to cook for another 5 minutes, then push everything through a sieve (or use a blender, in which case take out the thyme, bay leaf and lemon peel first). Season with pepper and a little lemon juice – salt will probably not be necessary because of the ham stock, but taste it and adjust if necessary. Return the mixture to the saucepan, adding a little more stock, if necessary. Whisk together the egg yolks with the cream and gradually add to the soup. Reheat gently – do not allow it to get too hot. Serve with croûtons or with small snippets of puff pastry baked golden brown.

Soup made with yellow split peas

6 oz (160g) yellow split peas
1¾ pints (1 litre) ham stock
sprig of thyme
1 medium-sized onion
2 or 3 medium-sized potatoes
1 small celeriac
1 tablespoon butter or pork
  dripping
1 small carton cream

Soak the peas overnight in cold water. Pour off the water and place the peas in a saucepan. Cover with the ham stock and add the thyme. Bring to the boil, lower the heat and simmer until the peas are tender.

Meanwhile peel and chop the onion. Peel and dice the potatoes and celeriac. Melt the butter or the dripping in a large saucepan, add the onion and allow it to soften. Add the potato and celeriac cubes and continue frying very gently until tender but still firm.

Press the peas through a sieve and reheat in the liquid in which they were cooked. Stir in the cream and reheat gently. Add the potatoes and celeriac. Check seasoning and serve. Small pieces of crisply fried bacon are a splendid addition; so is finely chopped ham.

Cheese soup

6 oz (170g) processed cheese
2 oz (60g) butter
1½ oz (40g) flour
1½ pints (800ml) good clear
  stock
salt and pepper
1 teaspoon caraway seeds
5 fl oz (140ml) cream
2 egg yolks
fresh chervil or marjoram

Slice or chop the cheese. Melt the butter in a saucepan, stir in the flour and allow to colour lightly. Gradually add the stock and the cheese, stirring all the time. Season with salt and pepper and caraway seeds. Cook over very low heat, stirring from time to time, until the cheese has melted completely. Whisk together the cream and egg yolks, pour in the hot soup gradually, whisking all the time. Reheat very gently – do not allow the soup to come to the boil, otherwise it will curdle. Serve sprinkled with finely chopped fresh chervil or marjoram or, failing that, with finely chopped fresh parsley.

You can of course ring the changes by using different kinds of cheese. Smoked processed cheese gives a completely different flavour, and a little finely chopped ham goes well with this too. There is also processed cheese with chives (sold in tubes) which is excellent too for this recipe, but in this case leave out the caraway seeds and herbs and instead sprinkle some finely chopped fresh chives over the top.

Gorgonzola soup

1 heaped tablespoon butter
1 small onion, finely chopped
2–3 fl oz (60–85ml) dry white wine
1 heaped tablespoon flour
1 heaped tablespoon finely chopped parsley

1¾ pints (1 litre) beef stock
4½ oz (125g) chopped or crumbled Gorgonzola cheese
salt and white pepper
chopped chives
fried croûtons

Melt the butter in a large saucepan. Add the chopped onion and simmer gently until transparent. Pour in the white wine and cook until the liquid is reduced to about half. Remove from the heat, stir in the flour and the chopped parsley. Return the saucepan to the heat and gradually pour in the stock. Blend well over low heat – a balloon whisk is best for this – and simmer for 10 minutes. Add the Gorgonzola cheese and allow to simmer for another 5 minutes. Season with white pepper and add a little more salt if necessary – taste the soup first. Sprinkle with chopped chives and serve with fried croûtons.

Cold starters – or party food

Some of my best herbs grow in a seed tray in my London bathroom: marjoram, chervil and basil – and tarragon too and even woodruff which is marvellous for making a wine cup (and the leaves twisted into a small wreath will scent your linen cupboard the whole year round). This is to prove that there is no excuse for resorting to those horrid dried herbs which taste faintly of hay and little else. Freeze-dried herbs are the best alternative to fresh herbs – except for deep-frozen herbs if you can get them. Treat them gently and allow time for them to recover – and above all, treat herbs with due deference, never mixing them indiscriminately or allowing one herb to dominate the others (a very little thyme or rosemary goes a long, long way – much further than the same quantity of basil or marjoram, for instance).

I might as well confess: I am completely and utterly hopeless when it comes to elaborately decorated food. Ask me to carve a radish into a rose and it will be my thumb that ends up in a funny shape. Probably because I disapprove of the whole operation and feel that any spare time and effort should be spent on preparing the food rather than on decorating it.

Not that I do not have a few 'party tricks' of my own – like cutting celeriac into matchstick strips and deep-frying them – to be handed round with drinks instead of potato crisps. Or my favourite Savoyard spread on squares of wholemeal or rye bread with a halved walnut on top . . .

For buffet suppers it may be something very simple like a tomato ring with a centre of chicken salad or a great big platter of vitello tonnato.

Tomato mousse

18 fl oz (500ml) tomato juice
pinch of sugar
juice of ½ lemon
1 packet Haco aspic jelly
½ pint (275ml) cream
  whipped to a soft peak

sprigs of watercress and
  lemon quarters for
  decoration

Gently heat the tomato juice with a pinch of sugar and the lemon juice to just below boiling point. Sprinkle in the aspic jelly and stir over a very low heat until the jelly has completely dissolved. Do not allow the mixture to come to the boil. Remove from the heat as soon as the jelly has dissolved and pour into a bowl to accelerate cooling. Put the bowl into the refrigerator as soon as the mixture is quite cold, and when it is just on the point of setting fold in the whipped cream. Make sure that the two mixtures are well blended. Rinse a mould, pile the mixture into this and leave to set. Turn out on to a serving dish and decorate with quartered lemons and sprigs of watercress. Delicious when served with thin slices of brown bread and butter and accompanied by a crisp salad.

Tomato ring

3 teaspoons (½ oz/15g)   salt and pepper
   powdered gelatine   pinch of sugar
18 fl oz (500ml) tomato juice   paprika
juice of ½ lemon   watercress

Put the gelatine in a cup and slake it with about 6 teaspoons of warm water, then stand the cup in a bowl of hot water and stir until the gelatine has dissolved completely. It should be quite clear and rather syrupy. Heat the tomato juice gently with all the seasonings to just below boiling point. Remove from the heat and stir in the dissolved gelatine. Continue stirring until well blended. Rinse a ring mould in cold water and pour in the tomato juice. Allow to cool and then put the mould into the refrigerator until the jelly has set completely. Turn out on to a pretty platter – it looks particularly good on a large glass plate – and garnish with watercress. Fill the centre with a salad – a rich creamy salad goes particularly well with the sharpness of the tomato jelly – hardboiled eggs sliced into mayonnaise with a sprinkling of chopped walnuts, for instance, or my favourite avocado salad (see page 123) or a light chicken salad (see page 127). Incidentally, by way of change, you can use V8 instead of tomato juice – or a mixture of both.

Egg *and mushroom mousse*

½ lb (225g) button
   mushrooms
1 lightly heaped tablespoon
   butter
salt and pepper
2 teaspoons powdered
   gelatine

4 hardboiled eggs
3–4 tablespoons mayonnaise
½ pint (275ml) cream
pinch of curry powder
slices of hardboiled egg and
   strips of green pepper for
   decoration

Clean and slice the mushrooms and simmer them gently in the
butter until they are cooked, then season with salt and pepper.
Leave to cool. Slake the powdered gelatine with about 6
teaspoons water in a cup, stand the cup in a bowl of hot water
and stir until the gelatine has dissolved completely. It should
be quite clear and rather syrupy in consistency. Mince the
hardboiled eggs and the mushrooms or use a blender or food
processor, but do not let the mixture get too smooth – there
should still be discernible little flecks of egg and mushroom
about. Add the mayonnaise and stir in the dissolved gelatine.
Whisk the cream until stiff, add a pinch of curry powder and
fold the whipped cream into the egg and mushroom mixture.
Taste and adjust the seasonings if necessary. Pile into a dish or
arrange in a mound on a platter and chill well until set.
Decorate with slices of hardboiled egg and strips of green
pepper or just sprinkle with a little paprika. The consistency of
this mousse is beautifully creamy which is as I like it. If you
prefer a mousse which can be set in a mould and then turned
out, more gelatine would have to be added and some of the
creaminess lost.

Eggs with chive sauce

Count two eggs per person if serving this as a supper dish, one egg if used as a starter. It looks very good arranged on a large platter, but make a slight indentation when masking the eggs with the sauce so that you know where to find the eggs – otherwise you are apt to break the yolks when serving. Alternatively, arrange the eggs in individual dishes.

4 eggs, poached
1 heaped tablespoon butter
1 flat tablespoon flour
¼ pint (140ml) milk
salt and white pepper
mace

¼ pint (140ml) cream
about 1 tablespoon
 Worcestershire sauce
2 heaped tablespoons
 chopped chives

Drain the poached eggs well and gently pat them dry with a paper towel. Melt the butter in a saucepan, stir in the flour and blend well. Do not allow the mixture to brown. Gradually stir in the milk and cook to a smooth paste. Season with salt, white pepper and a flick of mace (it is important to use white pepper for this, otherwise it will look like scattered cigarette ash). Set to cool and stir from time to time. Set the poached eggs on a serving dish or in individual dishes. Whisk the cream until stiff and fold into the cold sauce, together with the Worcestershire sauce and the chopped chives. Mask the eggs with the sauce and chill well before serving. Dark rye bread and butter is particularly good with this.

Creamy curried eggs

8 eggs
3–4 shallots
1 tablespoon butter
1 scant teaspoon curry
  powder
2 tablespoons ground or
  finely chopped almonds

2 5 fl oz/125ml cartons
  yoghourt
lettuce leaves
strips of pickled red pepper
  for decoration

Boil the eggs for 6–7 minutes – they should still be slightly soft inside (the exact time depends on their size and freshness). Rinse them in cold water and peel them. This is much easier than it sounds if you carefully peel a little 'belt' from the middle – the rest of the shell will then come away quite easily.

Finely chop the shallot. Melt the butter in a saucepan, add the chopped shallots and soften them in the butter over a low flame. Do not allow them to brown. When the onions are soft, add the curry powder – or mild curry paste – and allow it to froth up. Stir and remove the pan from the heat. Stir in the almonds and the yoghourt. Blend well. Leave to cool.

Arrange the eggs on a bed of crisp lettuce on a serving dish and mask them with the sauce. (Salt is not usually necessary – but taste the sauce first and decide for yourself.) Decorate with strips of pickled – or fresh – red pepper.

Stuffed eggs

6 hardboiled eggs
3 oz (80g) butter
pinch of salt and pepper
pinch of paprika

1 good teaspoon French
  mustard
a little cream
chopped chives

Halve the eggs, scoop out the yolks. Cream the butter with salt, pepper and paprika. Beat in the egg yolks and the French mustard. Add enough cream to give a thick, smooth consistency. Taste and adjust the seasoning if necessary. Pile the mixture into the halved egg whites (you could use a forcing bag to do this, but personally I think it is a waste of time) and sprinkle with chopped chives. Chill until required.

Vitello tonnato

a few veal bones
1–2 carrots
1 onion
a few celery tops
1 bay leaf
1 leek (green part only)
salt and peppercorns
a little grated nutmeg
1½–2 lb (675–900g) veal
  one piece, shoulder for
  preference

7 oz/196g tin tuna fish
lemon juice
mayonnaise
capers, slices of hardboiled
  egg and strips of red or
  green pepper for
  decoration

Put the veal bones, vegetables and seasonings into a large saucepan and more than cover with water. Bring to the boil and simmer gently for about half an hour. Add the veal – which should be completely covered by the liquid – and allow this to poach gently in the liquid for about 1 hour. Leave to get cold in the liquid.

Sieve the tuna fish (or use a blender), then beat in a little of the liquid in which the meat was cooked (the remainder makes superb stock), a little lemon juice and enough mayonnaise to give a thick, spreadable paste. Taste and adjust seasoning if necessary. Cut the veal into slices and assemble in one of the following ways:

1. Spread each slice with the tunny mixture and arrange the slices, overlapping slightly, on a large platter. Chill before serving.
2. Spread each slice on either side with the tunny mixture and then reassemble the meat into its original shape, spreading the remaining tunny paste over it. Cover and chill overnight. On the next day cut between the slices (dip the knife into hot water if necessary) and arrange them, spread fan-wise, on a serving dish.

Decorate the meat with capers and slices of hardboiled eggs as well as strips of red and green peppers.

Radishes with anchovy butter

This makes a rather pleasant dish for nibbling with drinks.

8 oz (225g) butter
4 oz (112g) anchovy fillets,
  scraped

red and white radishes
chopped chives
4 hardboiled eggs

Cream the butter with the scraped anchovies – or pass them through the blender – and put into the refrigerator to chill. When the butter has hardened, form it into a roll – dip your hands into cold water first to do this, and twist the roll into a ring. Set it on a plate, make a few incisions all round it with a sharp knife and fill the centre with small white and red radishes, leaving the small stalks still on them.

Sprinkle chopped chives round the outside of the ring and then make a pretty pattern with alternate small mounds of finely chopped hardboiled egg white and sieved egg yolk. Dip the radishes first into the anchovy butter and then into the chives and the eggs.

Ham rolls with green peppers and tomatoes

2 shallots or small onions	3 oz (85g) cooked rice
3 green peppers	3 oz (85g) grated Cheddar
3 large tomatoes	cheese
1 tablespoon oil	butter for the dish
salt	6 large slices ham
a small sprig of thyme	a little oil
pinch of powdered bay leaf	

Chop the shallots – or small onions – very finely. Cut the green peppers into strips, having removed the seeds and the stalks. Scald the tomatoes, then plunge them into cold water and remove the skins. Heat the oil in a frying pan, add the chopped onions and soften them in the oil, then turn up the heat and allow them to brown lightly. Add the green peppers, the quartered tomatoes, a pinch of salt, the sprig of thyme and a pinch of powdered bay leaf. (You can add a whole bay leaf, but

45

remember to remove it before the ham rolls are filled.) Cover the pan with a lid and leave to simmer until the peppers are soft. Stir in the cooked rice and the grated cheese. Remove the sprig of thyme.

Butter a gratin dish. Divide the tomato mixture between the slices of ham and spread each slice with the mixture – allow it to cool a little first. Roll up the ham slices and lay them, folded side underneath, in the buttered gratin dish. Brush over them with a little olive oil and bake for about 10 minutes at Gas Mark 6 (400°F). Serve hot or cold.

Picnic loaf

1 French loaf
8 oz (225g) butter
6 oz (170g) cooked ham
6 oz (170g) salami sausage
6 oz (170g) cooked tongue

2 oz (60g) Emmenthal or
  Gruyère cheese
2 hardboiled eggs
2 small pickled cucumbers
2–3 anchovies

The ingredients can be varied according to taste – use a few chopped black olives instead of the pickled cucumbers or add a dash of French mustard for extra flavour. After making this picnic loaf a few times you will no doubt start to create your own special version!

Cut both ends off the French loaf and scoop out all the soft crumb. This is not as difficult as it sounds, but it does require a bit of patience and the handle of a wooden cooking spoon. (If the French loaf is very long, cut it into two pieces of roughly the same size.)

Chop up all the ingredients except the anchovies and the butter. Do not use a mincer or a blender – it would give too fine a texture – just an ordinary chopping knife. Cream the butter, blend in the scraped anchovies and then gradually work in the other ingredients. Fill the hollowed-out loaf with this mixture, wrap it in foil and chill it overnight. Cut into fairly thin slices.

For a picnic, wrap the cut slices – reassembled – in foil and pack a few pickled cucumbers and crunchy celery stalks to eat with them.

Savoyard cheese

I first tasted this in a small Belgian restaurant – and was given the recipe on the spot. Delicious served on squares of wholemeal or rye bread with a halved walnut on top.

Just beat together equal quantities of creamed butter, ripe Camembert and Roquefort (or failing that, Dolcelatte) cheese until very smooth, then beat in a sprinkling of freshly ground black pepper and a dash of brandy or – as I was taught – 'a measure of the good red wine you should drink with it'.

Fish

The selection of fish dishes may seem a little one-sided at first – it is not only small, but there is also an abundance of recipes for fresh water fish. Pike and carp are much neglected and underrated in this country but they can be prepared in so many different and delicious ways – cooked with cream or in a light paprika sauce – which I feel are worth trying.

Not that I have neglected other fish entirely – there is my favourite Waterzooi of Flanders, not made with chicken as is more usual, but with turbot which I consider makes one of the best fish dishes ever (I did not invent it, but it is a dish which deserves being far better known), and my other favourite, turbot with fresh walnut butter which is so well worth waiting for until the walnuts are just ripe . . .

Carp cooked with cream

1 carp, about 3–4 lb
  (1½–2kg)
salt
white pepper
butter for the dish
1 lb (450g) potatoes

4 oz (110g) butter
½ pint (280ml) cream
  or sour cream
about 3 tablespoons fresh
  breadcrumbs

The whole secret of this dish, which is far more delicious than many more complicated recipes, lies in prejudging the length of time the fish and potatoes will take to cook so that they are both ready at the same time. This means gauging the correct thickness of the potato slices. New potatoes take surprisingly long when cooked this way, so slice them thinner than old potatoes.

Clean, wash and scale the carp, but leave it whole. Make three or four incisions on each side of the fish and rub well with salt and pepper. Butter a deep ovenproof dish. Scrape or peel the potatoes, slice them and arrange them in the dish. Dot with a third of the butter and sprinkle with salt and pepper. Pour about half the cream over the potatoes and place the carp on top. Pour the remaining cream over the fish and dot with half the remaining butter. Bake at Gas Mark 4 (350°F) for about 1 hour, basting frequently. Sprinkle the fish with the bread-crumbs, dot with the remaining butter. Increase the heat to Gas Mark 8 (450°F) and bake for a further few minutes, until nicely browned.

Carp or pike in paprika sauce

1 carp or pike, weighing about 2½ lb (1¼kg)
salt
1 very large onion
5 oz (140g) butter
1 tablespoon chopped parsley

¾ pint (425ml) cream
1 tablespoon paprika
2 egg yolks
1 tablespoon lemon juice
2 tablespoons chopped capers

Skin and fillet the fish and cut into pieces of about 1 inch by 2 inches. Sprinkle with salt and set aside until required. Peel and thinly slice the onion.

Melt the butter in a heavy saucepan, add the onion, parsley and the pieces of fish. Cover and simmer gently for 15 minutes. Add the cream and the paprika and simmer for a further 30 minutes. Lift out the fish and the onion and arrange on a warmed serving dish. Keep hot.

Strain the sauce from the pan into the top of a double boiler. Blend the egg yolks with the lemon juice and 1–2 tablespoons of the strained sauce. Stir into the remaining sauce in the double boiler and cook gently over steam until thickened. Add chopped capers and adjust seasoning if necessary. Pour over the fish and serve.

Cod cooked in beer the Flemish way

(serves 4)

butter for the dish
3 oz (90g) butter
6 oz (170g) onions cut into
  rings
salt
4 cod fillets, each weighing
  about 6–8 oz (170–225g)

seasoned flour
7 fl oz (200ml) strong lager
1 bay leaf
4 slices lemon
4 tablespoons fresh white
  breadcrumbs

Preheat the oven to Gas Mark 4 (350°F). Butter a deep gratin dish, large enough to take the cod fillets side by side. Melt a tablespoon of the butter and soften the onion rings in this. Cover the base of the gratin dish with the onion rings and sprinkle with a little salt.

Add a heaped tablespoon of the butter to the pan in which the onions were fried. Dust the fish fillets with the seasoned flour and fry them quickly on both sides. Transfer to the gratin dish. Swill out the pan with the beer and pour over the fish. Add the bay leaf. Dot the fish with the remaining butter and place a slice of lemon on each fillet. Bake for about 15 minutes.

Sprinkle the fillets with the breadcrumbs and bake for another 5 minutes. Remove the bay leaf before serving.

Fish gulyas

2 lb (900g) firm white fish
2 medium or 1 large onion
2 fl oz (60ml) olive oil
1 green pepper
salt and pepper

1 tablespoon paprika
about 1 cupful fish stock
1 tablespoon tomato purée
5 fl oz (140ml) sour cream

Cut the fish into fairly large pieces. Slice the onion finely. Heat the olive oil and soften the onion in this. Deseed the green pepper and cut it into strips. Add to the onion and simmer for another 5 minutes. Turn up the heat and brown onion, green pepper and the fish pieces together. Sprinkle with salt, pepper and the paprika. Carefully pour in the fish stock and add the tomato purée. Simmer very slowly until the fish is tender – do not stir, but just gently shake the pan from time to time. Finally, stir in the sour cream and simmer gently for another 4–5 minutes.

Salmon mousse

1 tablespoon butter
1 small onion or shallot,
  finely chopped
8 oz (225g) tomatoes,
  blanched, skinned and
  quartered
1 lb (450g) cooked fresh
  salmon
4 medium-sized eggs,
  separated

2 tablespoons cream
salt and white pepper
a few drops of Worcestershire
  sauce
1 tablespoon gelatine crystals
4 tablespoons medium-dry
  sherry
black olives and mayonnaise
  to garnish

Heat the butter in a saucepan, add the chopped onion or shallot and simmer gently until softened. Add the tomatoes and simmer for another 10–15 minutes, until reduced to a pulp and slightly thickened.

Remove skin and bone from the salmon and purée the flesh in a blender with the tomato and onion. Beat the egg yolks into the mixture together with the cream. Add the salt, pepper and Worcestershire sauce. Gently heat the gelatine in the sherry to dissolve and add to the purée. Whisk the egg whites until stiff and fold them into the fish mixture.

Pour the mixture into a lightly buttered pudding basin or mould. Chill until set (about 1½ hours).

To serve, dip the bowl briefly into hot water and turn out the mousse on to a serving dish. Garnish with black olives and mayonnaise.

Soufflé pancakes with prawns

2 eggs
2 oz (60g) butter
9 oz (250g) sieved cottage
  cheese
5 fl oz (140ml) sour cream
1 oz (30g) grated Parmesan
  cheese

4 oz (120g) cooked and
  peeled prawns
8 very thin pancakes, about
  6–7 inches in diameter
butter for the dish

Separate the egg yolks and whites. Preheat the oven to Gas
Mark 6 (400°F). Cream the butter until light and fluffy, then
beat in the egg yolks, one by one, and the cottage cheese.
Gradually add the sour cream. Whisk the egg whites until stiff
and fold into the mixture alternately with the grated Parmesan
cheese. Finally add the prawns. Spread a little of the mixture
down the centre of each pancake and fold it over lightly. Lay
each pancake – folded side downwards – in a buttered gratin
dish and bake until nicely puffed up – about 20 minutes. Serve
at once – it will collapse like any other soufflé if kept waiting.

Trout with mushrooms
(serves 4)

1 tablespoon butter
1 heaped tablespoon finely
  chopped onion
butter for the dish
4 trout
salt and pepper
a little lemon juice

1 glass white wine (dry)
1 heaped tablespoon butter
½ lb (225g) sliced button
  mushrooms
salt and white pepper
a little lemon juice
a good dash of cream

Melt a tablespoon of butter in a thick pan and gently soften the chopped onion in this. Butter a deep baking dish which has a well-fitting lid. Sprinkle the softened onion over the bottom of the baking dish.

Clean the trout, pat them dry and dust lightly with salt and pepper. Sprinkle with a little lemon juice. Lay the trout side by side in the baking dish. Pour the wine over them, put the lid on top and put the dish into the oven at Gas Mark 6 (400°F) until the trout are cooked – this obviously varies a little according to size, but it usually takes between 12 and 15 minutes.

Meanwhile melt a good tablespoon of butter in a pan and add the sliced button mushrooms. Simmer them very gently until they are just cooked – they should still have a little 'bite' to them. Season with salt, white pepper and a little lemon juice, stir and then add a good dash of cream. Stir again and then pour over the trout. Close the dish and return it to the oven for another 3–4 minutes, having turned up the heat to Gas Mark 7 (425°F). Serve at once.

Trout with cream sauce
(serves 4)

4 trout	1 heaped tablespoon each of
salt and pepper	chopped parsley and
flour	chives
butter for frying	8 fl oz (225ml) cream
1 heaped tablespoon butter	nutmeg

Clean the trout and pat dry very lightly. Sprinkle inside and out with salt and pepper and dust the outside with flour. Fry the trout very gently in butter and keep hot in a warmed serving dish.

Melt the butter in a frying pan, add the chopped parsley and chives. Blend well and pour in the cream. Stir and then pour into the pan in which the trout were cooked. Heat gently, stirring all the time. Add a little salt and a flick of nutmeg. Allow to thicken and then pour over the trout.

Turbot with fresh walnut butter
(serves 2)

This is one of the dishes I learned from Eckart Witzigmann at the 'Aubergine' in Munich. There are only a few weeks in the year when walnuts are fresh enough to be peeled and used in this dish. Worth waiting for though for the rest of the year . . .

2 thick turbot fillets weighing
   about ½ lb each (225g)
2 oz (50g) fresh shelled and
   skinned walnuts
2 oz (50g) butter

1 anchovy fillet
a little pepper
2 tablespoons unsweetened
   grape juice
butter for the foil

The walnuts have to be fresh enough for the thin brown skins to come away easily. Grind just over half of the walnuts very finely and chop the remainder coarsely. Cream the butter until fluffy, beat in the scraped anchovy fillet so that you have a light creamy mixture, then beat in the ground as well as the chopped walnuts. Season very lightly with pepper – no salt.

Butter two pieces of kitchen foil measuring about 10 by 12 inches, large enough to enclose the fillets with room to spare. Cut through the thickness of the fillets to within ¼ inch of the edge. Spread inside of each fillet with the anchovy and walnut butter and close the fillets again. Set each fillet on a sheet of buttered foil and sprinkle with grape juice. Close the foil over the fillet, leaving plenty of room. Set the parcels on a baking sheet and bake in a preheated oven at Gas Mark 4 (350°F) for about 20 minutes. Serve the parcels – unopened – on heated plates.

Waterzooi made with turbot

FOR THE FISH STOCK
3 oz (80g) butter
1–2 medium-sized onions, finely chopped
3–4 celery sticks, chopped
bones and trimmings from the turbot
10 fl oz (275ml) white wine
2 parsley roots
1 bay leaf
a little thyme
a little lemon peel – and juice
black peppercorns
salt

FOR THE WATERZOOI
2–3 medium-sized carrots
2–3 shallots
the white part of 3–4 leeks
2 oz (60g) butter
10 dill seeds
½ pint (275ml) cream
salt and pepper
4–6 turbot fillets, each weighing about 5–6 oz (about 150g) with trimmings and bones (about 150g)
2–3 threads saffron or a pinch of powdered saffron
chopped chervil or parsley

Melt the 3 oz butter, add the chopped vegetables and the fish bones and trimmings and soften in the hot butter for a few minutes without browning. Add the wine, parsley roots, bay leaf, thyme, lemon peel and juice, the peppercorns, salt and 1½ pints (800ml) water. Slowly bring the liquid to the boil and simmer for 30–40 minutes. Remove from heat and strain.

Grate or finely chop the carrots and shallots. Finely shred the leeks. Melt the butter in a large thick saucepan, add the vegetables and the dill seeds and cook gently for about 10 minutes. Add the fish fillets and 1½ pints (800ml) of the strained stock. Cook gently over low heat until the fish is tender, but still firm. Lift out the fish and keep warm in a deep heated dish. Add cream and saffron and blend well over low heat until just slightly thickened. Pour over the fish and serve in deep soup plates, sprinkled with a little chopped chervil or parsley.

Meat

Beef cooked in beer
(serves 6)

2¼–3¼ lb (1.1–1.6kg) good
stewing steak
salt and pepper
4–5 oz (110–140g) good
dripping or lard
2 scant oz (50g) flour
1 lb (450g) onions, chopped
9 oz (250g) green streaky
bacon, diced

2 bottles strong lager or
light ale
a sprig of thyme
1 bay leaf
1 tablespoon brown sugar
1 tablespoon wine vinegar

Preheat the oven to Gas Mark 9 (475°F). Cut the beef into large bite-sized pieces and season with salt and pepper. Melt the lard or dripping in a large frying pan and fry the meat – in batches if necessary – until lightly browned on both sides. Transfer the meat into a casserole dish with a slotted spoon, sprinkle with the flour and mix well. Put the uncovered casserole into the oven for about 5 minutes.

Meanwhile brown the chopped onion in the same pan as the meat. Add the bacon, stir and then add onions and bacon to the meat. Pour the lager over the meat, add the thyme, bay leaf, sugar and vinegar. Cover the casserole with a lid and return to the oven at Gas Mark 3 (325°F). Cook until meat is tender – 1½–2 hours.

Summer casserole

1½–2 lb (675–900g) stewing
  steak
2 tablespoons olive oil
1 large onion, sliced
1 green pepper
1 red pepper
4 courgettes, sliced

1 lb very small potatoes,
  scrubbed and dried
4 large tomatoes, skinned and
  chopped
salt and pepper
a few basil leaves
½ teaspoon coriander seeds

Best cooked in a flameproof casserole which can be brought straight to the table. Cut the stewing steak into squares or strips. Heat the oil in a thick flameproof casserole and quickly seal the meat in this. Keep the meat warm. Now soften the sliced onion in the same oil, adding a little more if necessary. Add the peppers, deseeded and destalked and cut into strips, and soften them with the onion over low heat. Add the sliced courgettes – no need to peel them – turn up the heat and brown everything together. Add the potatoes, leaving them whole. Stir, then add the tomatoes. Add the meat, salt, pepper, the basil and the coriander seeds. Stir and cover with a lid, then put the casserole into the oven at Gas Mark 3 (325°F) until the meat is tender – about 1–1½ hours. Extra liquid should not be required, but check from time to time and add only if necessary.

Hunter's loaf

1 tablespoon lard or good
dripping
2 rashers bacon, derinded
and chopped
1 small onion, finely chopped
1 crushed clove garlic
1 tablespoon chopped
parsley
2 day-old rolls
1 lb (450g) lean minced beef
1 lb (450g) minced pork

salt and pepper
chopped marjoram
flour or fine breadcrumbs
2–3 hardboiled eggs
bacon rashers
1 small onion
1–2 slices celeriac
1 tablespoon chopped capers
1 carton (5 fl oz/140ml) sour
cream

Melt the lard or dripping in a frying pan, add the chopped
bacon and fry very gently for a few minutes. Add the finely
chopped onion and the garlic and fry until everything is lightly
browned. Stir in the parsley and set aside.

Soak the rolls in water (or milk) until softened and squeeze
out all moisture. (If they are crusty rolls it is best to grate off
the rind first.) Add the rolls to the meat and also add the onion
mixture from the pan, together with salt, pepper and a little
chopped marjoram. Mix everything together well – the best
way to do this is to knead the mixture like dough, dipping your
hands into cold water from time to time. When the mixture is
very smooth, flatten it out on a kitchen table or pastry board
previously sprinkled with flour or fine breadcrumbs. Put two
or three hardboiled eggs down the centre and fold the meat
mixture over it, shaping it into a loaf. Put the loaf into a
roasting tin and cover the top with overlapping strips of bacon.

Add a small onion and 1–2 slices of celeriac and roast for 1–
1½ hours at Gas Mark 5 (375°F). Basting should not be
necessary as the fat from the bacon will see to that. Carefully
lift the loaf from the pan and set it on a warmed dish.

Pour off the fat from the pan and discard the onion and the slices of celeriac. Pour in about a cupful of water – or good stock – and bring to the boil, stirring up all the residue from the pan. Allow to boil fiercely until reduced to about half, then stir in the sour cream and the chopped capers and reheat gently. Serve the sauce separately.

Marjoram tokany
(serves 2–3)

1 lb (450g) lean beef
1 medium-sized onion
2 tablespoons oil or good
  dripping
salt and pepper

finely chopped marjoram
3 fl oz (85ml) white wine
5 oz (140g) bacon
8 fl oz (225ml) sour cream

Cut the beef into strips and flatten them a little with the knife as you go along. Slice the onion thinly. Heat the oil or the dripping in a thick saucepan and fry the onion until it is golden brown. Throw in the sliced meat, stir, then add salt, pepper and a generous measure of finely chopped fresh marjoram. Turn down the heat and moisten the meat with the wine. Cover with a lid and simmer very gently until the meat is about half cooked. In the meantime dice the bacon and fry or grill it lightly. Add the bacon to the meat, stir and then add the sour cream. Replace the lid on the saucepan and leave to cook very gently until the meat is tender. Adjust seasoning if necessary and add another dollop of sour cream before serving. Fluffy mashed potatoes go particularly well with this dish.

Casserole of meat balls

1 medium-sized onion
1½ lb (675g) good stewing
  steak
1–2 tablespoons oil
salt and pepper
1 tablespoon finely chopped
  fresh herbs

1–2 slices bread (optional)
a little beaten egg (optional)
1 lb (450g) well-scrubbed
  small potatoes
2 skinned tomatoes

Chop the onion finely. Mince the stewing steak – I prefer doing this to buying ready-minced beef which is usually too fatty. Heat the oil in a casserole, add half the chopped onion and allow it to soften in the oil. Season the minced meat with salt and pepper and add the chopped herbs (lovage is particularly good if you can get it). Mix well. If you want to 'stretch' the quantity, add one or two slices of bread, previously soaked in a little cold water, with all the moisture squeezed out. Work in the remaining chopped onion and if you have used bread, add a little beaten egg for binding. Shape the mixture into mounds about the size of a table-tennis ball. Turn up the heat under the onions and brown them and the meat balls together. Add the well-scrubbed potatoes and brown these lightly too, adding a little more oil if necessary. Sprinkle with salt and pepper and broken-up tomatoes.

Cover the casserole with a lid and put it into the oven at Gas Mark 3 (325°F) until the potatoes are cooked, adding water in the smallest possible quantity and only if strictly necessary. I do not thicken the gravy at all since I prefer it in its 'natural' state, but if you like thicker gravy, brown about a tablespoon flour with the onions and the meat – but you will have to add more liquid while cooking.

If you have a food processor, the whole procedure is

simpler still: chop the onion in the food processor and take out half to soften in the hot oil. While this is happening, add the meat to the onion in the food processor, together with seasonings and herbs. Do not over-process it, otherwise the meat balls will be too smooth.

Casserole of sweetbreads
(serves 4 as a first course or 2 as a main course)

1 lb (450g) calves' sweetbreads
salt
dash of wine vinegar
2 tablespoons butter
½ lb (225g) button mushrooms
1 small onion

1 lightly heaped tablespoon flour
7 fl oz (200ml) chicken stock
salt and pepper
sprig of thyme
a little marjoram
a little chopped lovage
3 tablespoons cream

Put the sweetbreads into a bowl and cover with cold water to which a good pinch of salt and a few drops of wine vinegar have been added. Leave to soak for several hours, changing the water from time to time and always adding salt and vinegar as before. Three hours will do nicely: the sweetbreads should be creamy white by then. Pull off as much of the outer skin as possible as you change the water, taking care not to damage the meat.

Plunge the sweetbreads into boiling salt water to which a few drops of wine vinegar have been added and poach them very gently for a few minutes, then rinse them under a cold tap. Now carefully pull off all the remaining outer skin and cut the sweetbreads into pieces about the size of a small button mushroom. Melt the butter in a pan, lightly fry the sweetbreads in this and then transfer them to a casserole. Fry the cleaned button mushrooms in the same fat and add them to the sweetbreads in the casserole. (If some of the mushrooms are too large, halve or quarter them, but I prefer to leave them whole when possible.) Finely chop the onion and soften it in the same fat, adding a little more butter if necessary. Dust with flour, stir, and let the flour brown a little, then swill out the pan with the stock and pour over the sweetbreads and mushrooms. Season with salt and pepper and add a sprig of thyme, a little marjoram and a little chopped lovage. Put the casserole into the oven at Gas Mark 3–4 (325–350°F) for about 1 hour, by which time the sauce should be nice and creamy. Remove the casserole lid towards the end of the cooking time to accelerate the thickening. Remove the thyme and marjoram, stir in the cream and simmer for another few minutes before serving.

Pork escalopes with apples and Calvados
(serves 2)

2 large or 4 smaller pork
   escalopes
about 1 tablespoon flour
1 heaped tablespoon butter
1 tablespoon oil
1 large onion, finely sliced

2 large apples, peeled, cored
   and finely sliced
good dash Calvados
salt and pepper
a little marjoram

Trim the escalopes and make a few incisions round the edges. Wipe the escalopes with a paper towel, then dust them lightly with the flour on both sides. Heat the oil and butter in a thick frying pan and brown the escalopes on both sides. Transfer them to a casserole dish. Throw the sliced onion into the hot oil and butter, stir and then add the sliced apples. Brown the apples and onions in the butter and oil, then add them to the escalopes. Swill out the frying pan with a good dash of Calvados and remember to stir up all the bits from the bottom of the pan. Pour over the escalopes. Season with salt, pepper and a little marjoram. Cover casserole with a lid and put it into the oven at Gas Mark 4 (350°F) for about 30–40 minutes. Fluffy mashed potatoes go particularly well with this dish.

Pork escalopes with bacon
(serves 4)

4 lean pork escalopes	salt
French mustard	1 heaped tablespoon clarified
4 slices bacon, derinded	butter
powdered rosemary or sprigs	2–3 tablespoons dry white
of rosemary	wine

Flatten the pork escalopes and make a few incisions round the edges to stop them from curling. Spread one side of each escalope thinly with French mustard and then cover with a thin slice of bacon, trimmed to size. Fasten with a wooden cocktail stick – simply slot it through. Dust with a little powdered rosemary or slot a small sprig of rosemary between the cocktail stick and the bacon. Dust the other side of the escalope lightly with salt. Heat the clarified butter in a frying pan and put in the escalopes, bacon side down. Fry until the bacon is brown and crisp, then turn over the escalopes and fry them until they are cooked, shaking the pan gently from time to time. Arrange the escalopes on a warmed serving dish. Pour the wine into the frying pan, bring to the boil and stir up all the sediment in the pan. Pour the juices over the escalopes and serve at once.

Pork in spiced beer sauce
(serves 2–3)

2 medium-sized onions
1 lb (450g) pork – shoulder
  for preference
1 heaped tablespoon butter
  or 2 tablespoons oil
salt

coarsely crushed black
  peppercorns
2 teaspoons caraway seeds
1 pint (575ml) lager
about 3 heaped tablespoons
  soft brown breadcrumbs

The darker the bread for the breadcrumbs, the better the dish.

Chop the onions finely. Cut the meat into convenient pieces. Heat the butter – or the oil – and lightly brown the chopped onion in this. When the onion has browned, sprinkle in some salt and pepper (I use coarsely crushed peppercorns rather than finely ground pepper) and the caraway seeds and stir. Add the meat and stir until the meat is sealed, but not browned, then pour in the beer. Cover with a lid and simmer very gently – on top of the stove – for half an hour. Sprinkle with the breadcrumbs, cover again with a lid and put the dish into the oven at Gas Mark 3 (325°F) for about an hour – until the meat is tender. Jacket potatoes go rather well with this dish.

Smoked loin of pork
baked in cheese pastry
(serves 6–8)

Smoked loin of pork is now widely available and, treated in this particular way, makes a very festive dish.

3½ lb (1.6kg) boned smoked loin of pork
2 oz (50g) butter
1 large onion, chopped
10 oz (275g) mushrooms, sliced

1 tablespoon chopped parsley
salt and pepper
2 eggs, lightly beaten

FOR THE PASTRY
8 oz (225g) plain flour
pinch salt
pinch nutmeg

8 oz (225g) butter
8 oz (225g) cottage cheese
beaten egg for glazing

Score lightly across the pork fat and then roast it at Gas Mark 6 (400°F) allowing 20 minutes per pound. (The instructions usually say that you should also allow 15–20 minutes over, but ignore this in this particular instance.) Set aside to cool.

Heat the butter, add the chopped onion and allow to soften in the butter. Add the sliced mushrooms and the chopped parsley and simmer gently until the mushrooms are cooked. Add salt and pepper to taste. Remove from heat and cool slightly, then stir in the lightly beaten eggs. Chill before use.

For the pastry, sift together the flour, salt and nutmeg. Cut the butter into the flour and then crumble the cottage cheese into the mixture, working as quickly and as lightly as possible. Pat into a round, cover and chill for at least 30 minutes.

Roll out the pastry on a lightly floured board to about ¼

inch thickness – large enough to enclose the meat. Put a thin layer of the mushroom mixture in the centre, then place the pork on top and cover the top and sides with the remaining mushroom mixture. Wrap completely in the pastry and brush the joins with lightly beaten egg before sealing firmly. Cut away any uneven edges of pastry and use these for decoration or to cover the pastry joins. Brush with lightly beaten egg and set on a baking sheet previously rinsed with cold water. Bake in a preheated oven at Gas Mark 6 (400°F) for about 30–40 minutes. Set on a warmed platter and allow to rest for about 10 minutes before carving.

Bean pot

1 lb (450g) small dried white beans
1 large onion
1 heaped tablespoon lard or good dripping
1–2 crushed garlic cloves
a sprig each of thyme and rosemary
a little winter savory
dash of wine vinegar
1 tablespoon soft brown sugar
1 tablespoon tomato ketchup
1 dessertspoon Dijon mustard
a few peppercorns
2–3 small knuckles of smoked pork
tomato juice
about 10 slices of spiced sausage
6–8 bacon rashers

Soak the beans in cold water overnight. Pour away the water the next day and rinse the beans under a cold running tap.

Chop the onion coarsely. Heat the lard or the dripping in a thick casserole dish, throw in the chopped onion and the crushed garlic and allow them to soften over low heat. Add the beans, thyme, rosemary and winter savory. Stir, then add a dash of wine vinegar, the sugar, tomato ketchup, mustard and the peppercorns – but no salt. Pour in enough tomato juice to cover the beans and put the smoked knuckles of pork on top (ends of bacon joints are ideal for this dish and most shops selling bacon have them, but they have to be asked for as a rule). Add the sliced sausage – it can be anything from small chunks of Cabanos to well-spiced garlic sausage from Marks and Spencers, but the emphasis is on 'well-spiced'. Cover the casserole first with kitchen foil and then with the lid for a really close fit. Put into a fairly low oven – Gas Mark 3 (325°F) – to cook very gently until the beans are tender and the knuckles of pork practically fall to bits. If necessary add a little more tomato juice during the cooking time – I prefer this to adding stock, but you can add stock if you like, or a mixture of stock and tomato juice – it is simply a matter of personal preference. Taste for seasoning and if necessary add a little salt and also a bit more sugar or vinegar. Sometimes I add the bacon – derinded and the bacon rinds tied together and cooked with the beans (to be fished out before serving) – during the last hour of cooking, but as a rule I grill them and serve the crisply grilled bacon on top of the bean pot, and I am not averse to grilling a few slices of garlic sausage and adding these as well. Serve with hunks of French bread.

Veal cakes
(serves 3–4)

5 fl oz (140ml) water
1 heaped tablespoon butter
pinch of salt
2 oz (60g) flour
1 egg
¾ lb (350g) pie veal

salt and pepper
nutmeg
butter or clarified butter for
  frying
a little clear stock
a small knob of butter

Put the water, the tablespoon of butter and the salt into a small saucepan and bring slowly to the boil, then tip in the flour. Stir over a low flame until the mixture leaves the sides of the saucepan clean. Remove from the fire and beat in the egg. Allow to cool, add the veal and then push the mixture twice through the mincer or food processor until smooth. Season with salt, pepper and a little grated nutmeg. Hold your hands under a cold running tap for a second or two, shake off the surplus water and then shape the meat mixture into small cakes, rather like hamburgers. Set them on a flat plate and leave them in a cold place or the refrigerator for about an hour. Heat a little oil or butter or – better still – clarified butter in a frying pan and fry the meat cakes slowly until they are nicely browned on both sides. Add about a ladleful of good clear stock, cover with a lid and leave to simmer for another 5 minutes or so. Arrange the meat cakes on a warmed platter, reduce the liquid in the pan to about half, add a small knob of butter, swish it around the pan and then pour over the meat cakes.

Braised pork tenderloin

2 whole pork tenderloins,
   about 2½ lb (1.1kg)
sprig of thyme
2 bay leaves
2–3 parsley roots
1 clove garlic
salt
crushed peppercorns
grated nutmeg

7 fl oz (200ml) red wine
1 tablespoon olive oil
2 oz (60g) butter
1 tablespoon Dijon mustard
1 tablespoon redcurrant jelly
dash of wine vinegar
1 teaspoon arrowroot (or
   potato flour)

Put the pork into a deep dish. Add thyme, bay leaves and parsley roots. Crush the garlic with a little salt and add, as well as the salt, a few crushed peppercorns and the nutmeg. Pour over the wine and the olive oil. Cover and leave in a cool place for two days, turning the meat over from time to time.

Take out the meat and dry it with kitchen paper. Reserve the marinade. Preheat the oven to Gas Mark 5 (375°F). Melt half the butter in a large baking dish, add the meat and seal on all sides. Cover the dish with foil and put the dish into the oven. Cook until meat is tender – this depends on the thickness of the tenderloins and should take about 20–25 minutes, but check after the first 15 minutes. Put the meat on a warmed serving dish and keep hot. Strain the marinade into the baking tin. Put the tin over direct heat and stir to take up all the sediment. Cook until the liquid is reduced by about a quarter. Stir in the mustard, the redcurrant jelly and a dash of wine vinegar. Slake the arrowroot with about 2 tablespoons of water and stir into the mixture. Stir into the marinade and simmer gently until thickened. Stir in the remaining butter in small flakes. Strain the sauce if necessary and pour a little of it over the sliced pork. Serve remainder separately.

Herb escalopes
(serves 4)

1 medium-sized onion, finely
  chopped
6 oz (170g) finely minced
  pork
2 tablespoons finely chopped
  parsley
a little chopped thyme and
  marjoram
salt and pepper
2 eggs

fine breadcrumbs
8 small pork escalopes
2 tablespoons butter
1 cup good stock
1 scant tablespoon flour
2 tablespoons chopped
  capers
salt and pepper
5 fl oz (140ml) sour cream

Add the chopped onion to the minced pork, then work in the chopped parsley, thyme and marjoram. Season with salt and pepper. Work in the eggs and just enough fine breadcrumbs to give a fairly loose mixture. Cover and leave to stand in a cool place for about 20 minutes, by which time the mixture will have thickened a little.

Flatten the pork escalopes with a rolling pin or a meat cleaver and spread each escalope with a little of the minced pork mixture. Roll up the escalopes and fasten each roll with a small wooden skewer – a wooden cocktail stick will do nicely. Brown the little rolls in the butter on all sides – I use a thick frying pan which will hold them side by side – then add a scant cupful of good stock. Cover with a lid and leave to simmer very gently until the meat is tender. Lift out the meat and keep warm on a hot serving dish.

Sprinkle the flour over the residue in the pan, stir and then add the capers and the sour cream. Stir to take up all the scrapings from the pan and cook gently until thickened. Adjust seasoning if necessary and pour over the meat.

Glazed ham with crackling
(serves 6–7)

1 ham or gammon joint,
  weighing about 3–4 lb
  (1.3–1.8kg)
a few peppercorns
1 medium-sized onion
1 bay leaf
1 tablespoon sugar
a few celery tops

cloves
about ½–¾ cup brown sugar
pinch of dry mustard powder
2 wineglassfuls red wine
juice of 1 orange and 1
  teaspoon grated orange
  rind
1 tablespoon redcurrant jelly

Soak the ham or gammon overnight in cold water, changing the water at least once. (I am not suggesting that you should get up in the middle of the night to attend to the ham, but if you put the ham to soak at around nine in the evening, you can change the water before you go to bed and again in the morning.)

Drain off the water, put the ham into a large saucepan, cover with fresh cold water and add the peppercorns, onion, bay leaf and the sugar, as well as the celery tops. Cover the saucepan and bring to the boil slowly, then leave to simmer gently, allowing 20 minutes to the pound – no more. Leave the ham to cool in the liquid until it is easy to handle.

Preheat the oven to Gas Mark 6 (425°F). Put the ham into a large baking dish. Peel off the rind and set aside, Score the surface of the ham into squares with a sharp knife and stud with cloves. Mix together enough brown sugar with a good pinch of dry mustard to cover the surface of the ham, and spread over it. Cut the rind into squares or strips and put these around the ham in the dish. Bake for about 8 minutes, then pour a wineglassful of red wine over the ham and bake for another 15–18 minutes, until the ham is nicely glazed and the crackling all crisp and crunchy and featherlight. Lift out the ham and set it on a heated serving dish, surrounded by the crackling. Pour off all the fat from the pan, add the remaining red wine to the residue in the pan, together with the orange juice and the grated orange peel. Stir over fierce heat, taking up all the scrapings in the pan. Add the redcurrant jelly and stir until slightly thickened. Serve separately.

As a rule I put some small scraped potatoes into the same baking dish – if they are small enough they take no more than 18–20 minutes – to bake with the ham. Otherwise I parboil them and just finish them off in the oven. They can of course be baked in a separate baking dish, together with the crackling, if the ham is very large and there is no room for them around the ham. And incidentally, the stock in which the ham was cooked makes beautiful soup!

Chicken in anchovy sauce

1 good-sized chicken or
   capon
a generous pint (600ml) good
   stock or a mixture of stock
   and dry white wine
1½ oz (40g) butter
5–6 scraped anchovy fillets
a little grated lemon rind

juice of ½ lemon
2 heaped tablespoons finely
   chopped parsley
5 tablespoons cream
a good tablespoon butter
a scant tablespoon flour
seasoning if necessary

Cut the chicken into six pieces (into eight if using a capon). I use rather sharp kitchen scissors for this. You can of course also prepare the dish with ready jointed chicken pieces.

Poach the chicken pieces very gently in the stock – or mixture of stock and white wine – until tender.

While this is happening, cream the butter until fluffy, then beat in the scraped anchovies, lemon rind and juice and the chopped parsley. If you have a food processor, just put all these ingredients – the parsley need be coarsely chopped only – into it and let it run until you have a smooth paste. Gradually beat in the cream.

As soon as the chicken pieces are tender – do not allow them to overcook – lift them out, remove the skin and keep warm on a deep serving dish.

Melt the butter in a saucepan, stir in the flour and allow to colour just slightly. Gradually add the strained liquid in which the chicken pieces have been cooked and stir over a low flame until the mixture has thickened. Add the anchovy mixture very gradually – a small spoonful at a time – and blend well. Do not allow the sauce to come to the boil. Pour over the chicken pieces and serve at once.

Chicken and chicory casserole

3–4 oz (85–110g) butter
1 crushed garlic clove
2 medium-sized onions,
  chopped
1 chicken weighing about
  3½ lb (about 1.6kg) with its
  liver

salt and pepper
2¼ lb (1kg) chopped chicory
grated nutmeg

Melt a scant tablespoon of the butter and lightly soften the crushed garlic and a tablespoon of the chopped onion in this. Lift out with a slotted spoon and add to the chopped chicken liver. Add salt and pepper to taste. Gently lift the chicken skin covering the breast and spread the mixture between skin and flesh. Truss the chicken and rub over lightly with salt and pepper.

Melt some more of the butter in the same pan in which the onions were softened and brown the chicken on all sides. Transfer the chicken to a casserole. Add the remaining butter and chopped onion and brown very lightly, then stir in the chopped chicory. Turn the heat to low and simmer very gently for about 8–10 minutes. Season with salt, pepper and a little nutmeg and add to the chicken. Swill out the pan with half a cup of water (or white wine) and pour over the chicken and chicory.

Cover the casserole and put it into the oven at Gas Mark 3 (325°F) until the chicken is tender – between 1 and 1½ hours, depending on size. Remove the chicken from the casserole, cut into joints and keep hot. Turn up the heat under the casserole to reduce any moisture to a glaze. Arrange the chicory on a warmed serving dish and put the chicken pieces on top.

Paprika chicken

1 chicken	dash of wine vinegar
1 green or red pepper	salt and pepper
2 tablespoons oil or 2 heaped tablespoons butter	1 teaspoon ground caraway seeds
1 large onion, finely chopped	5 fl oz (140ml) sour cream
1 heaped tablespoon paprika	

Wash and wipe the chicken and cut into convenient pieces. Deseed the pepper and cut it into strips or squares. Heat the oil or the butter in a thick saucepan, then throw in the sliced onion. Turn down the heat and leave the onion to simmer until soft, then turn up the heat and add the pepper. Fry until the onions are golden brown. Add the paprika, stir once or twice and then add about half a cupful of water and a dash of wine vinegar. Leave to simmer until well blended – about 2 or 3 minutes. Add the chicken pieces, salt, pepper and caraway seeds and stir so that the chicken pieces are well covered with the onion and paprika. Cover with a lid and leave to cook very gently either on top of the stove or in the oven at Gas Mark 3 (325°F) until the chicken is cooked, adding water only if this is absolutely necessary.

Just before serving add the sour cream, stir and cook gently until thickened. I do not thicken the sauce other than with the sour cream, but this is a question of personal taste – if you like, you can slake a scant dessertspoon of flour with a little of the liquid in which the chicken is cooking (or with the sour cream) and add it to the juices in the dish, then leave to cook gently for another 10 minutes. For a really smooth finish you may want to push the sauce through a sieve or swish it through a blender or food processor, but personally I think that this is gilding the lily!

Chicken livers in red wine sauce

1 lb (450g) chicken livers
approx. ½ pint (275ml) red wine
a little flour
approx. 2 tablespoons butter
salt and pepper
dash of brandy
2–3 tablespoons cream

Clean the chicken livers and cut off any discoloured bits. Cut the livers into slices, put them into a bowl and cover with red wine. Leave for about half an hour.

Drain the livers, retaining the liquid, and pat them dry with kitchen towelling. Dust very lightly with flour. Fry the sliced livers in hot butter – do not overcook them – then take them out with a slotted spoon. Keep the livers on a warmed dish.

Pour the wine in which the livers were marinaded into the pan, and stir to take up all the bits from the pan. Cook briskly until reduced and thickened, then add salt, pepper and a dash of brandy. Add the cream, reduce the heat and cook until well blended, then add the chicken livers and allow to simmer for a few minutes before serving.

Lamb ragout
(serves 4)

1–1¼ lb (500–600g) lean lamb
1 crushed bay leaf
1 teaspoon chopped marjoram
½ teaspoon finely crushed rosemary
¼ teaspoon finely crushed thyme
¼ teaspoon curry powder
a little freshly ground black pepper

1 large onion
1 clove garlic
1 bay leaf
4 oz (110g) carrots, grated
4 oz (110g) celeriac, grated
2–3 tablespoons oil or lard
1 tablespoon flour
a little good meat stock
dash of red wine

Dice the meat, sprinkle with the herbs, curry powder and pepper. Cover and set aside in a cool place overnight.

Peel and chop the onion. Crush the garlic. Heat the oil or lard in a saucepan and add onion and garlic. Simmer until softened, then allow it to brown lightly. Add the meat, bay leaf and the grated carrots and celeriac. Brown everything together very gently for about 20 minutes without adding any liquid, then add the flour and stir. Moisten with stock, adding a little at a time, and simmer for another 15–20 minutes. Take out the meat and keep hot. Sieve the residue remaining in the pan into another saucepan, add a dash of wine and adjust seasoning if necessary. Cook gently to thicken and then pour over the meat.

Leg of lamb in marinade

1 leg of lamb weighing about
   3½ lb (1.6kg)
25 fl oz (700ml) dry red wine
dash of red wine vinegar
6 juniper berries
1 teaspoon peppercorns
a little thyme
1–2 bay leaves
1 onion or 2 shallots, sliced
4–5 cloves
1 sliced carrot

½ sliced leek
a sprig rosemary
1–2 tablespoons oil
salt
a pinch of powdered ginger
1 tablespoon butter
1 scant tablespoon flour
1 teaspoon sugar
about 4 tablespoons sour
   cream

Put the wine, vinegar, vegetables, spices and herbs into a saucepan, bring slowly to the boil, simmer for about 4 minutes, then leave to cool in a covered saucepan. Put the meat into a casserole just large enough to hold the meat and the marinade. Pour the marinade over the meat, cover and leave in a cold place for 4–5 days, turning the meat over from time to time.

Take out the meat and pat it dry with kitchen towelling. Heat the oil in a large flameproof casserole and brown the meat on all sides. Strain the marinade over the meat and add salt and ginger. Cover the casserole and put it into the oven at Gas Mark 4 (350°F) and cook, turning the meat from time to time. The exact time will depend on how you like your lamb cooked.

Carve the meat into thick slices and arrange them on a

serving dish. Melt the butter in a saucepan, stir in the flour and the sugar and allow to brown. Pour on the juice from the meat and simmer until thickened. Stir in the sour cream and reheat gently. Serve the sauce separately.

Stuffed leg of lamb
(serves 6–8)

about 3½ lb (1.6kg) leg of
   lamb, boned but not rolled
1 clove garlic
salt and pepper

pinch of curry powder
powdered rosemary or sprig
   of fresh rosemary
1 pig's caul

FOR THE STUFFING
1 large onion
2 cloves garlic
2 oz (60g) streaky bacon
small pinch of powdered
   rosemary

fresh marjoram, thyme and
   crushed coriander seeds
10 oz (280g) lean minced
   pork and veal, mixed
salt and pepper

Remove and discard any surplus fat from the lamb. Peel and halve the clove of garlic and rub it over the surface of the meat. Mix together the salt, pepper, curry powder and powdered rosemary and rub over the meat as well. If using fresh rosemary make a few incisions in the meat and push in some of the rosemary.

To make the stuffing, peel and chop the onion. Peel and crush the garlic. Dice the bacon and finely chop the fresh herbs. Mix together the minced pork and veal with the onion, garlic, bacon, herbs and season with salt and pepper. Stuff this mixture into the boned leg of lamb and sew up the opening. Wrap the meat in the pork caul and place in a roasting tin.

Roast at Gas Mark 5 (375°F) for 1–1¼ hours for rare or 2 hours for well done, basting frequently.

Spatchcock poussins

1 plump little poussin per person

1 heaped tablespoon butter per poussin

salt and pepper

a good pinch paprika per poussin

a small pinch dry mustard per poussin

a small pinch curry powder per poussin (optional)

1 teaspoon tomato purée per poussin (optional)

Clean the poussins well, pat them dry with a kitchen towel and then split them down the back with a sharp knife or with kitchen scissors. Press down the breastbone – this is easiest done just with the palm of your hand – so that the poussins are fairly flat. Trim off the wing tips – they can go into the stockpot.

Put the butter into a small bowl and set it over steam or in a warm place to melt. Add salt, pepper, paprika and the dry mustard. (Sometimes I add also a little curry powder and about a teaspoon of tomato purée for each poussin.) Mix well and then brush the poussins with this mixture. Put the poussins under a hot grill and grill on both sides until cooked – this varies according to their size and also to the thickness of the meat. Cut through the breastbone before serving.

If the grill – or grill pan – if not large enough, or if you are trying to cook more poussins than it will comfortably hold, they can also be cooked in the oven. Simply put them on a rack in a large baking tin – or several baking tins for that matter – skin side up and roast them at Gas Mark 6 (400°F), brushing them with the melted butter mixture as they are cooking.

81

The juices in the pan make a delectable sauce, too: just add a little stock, bring to the boil, stirring up all the sediments in the pan, and then add a little thick cream and reheat gently.

Tarragon chicken

1 roasting chicken	paprika
butter	1 cup chicken stock
fresh tarragon	dash of brandy
salt	6 fl oz cream

Wash the chicken and pat it dry with kitchen paper. Gently loosen the skin around the breast of the chicken and slip a large knob of butter and a sprig of tarragon between skin and flesh on either side of the chicken breast. Put a sprig of tarragon inside the chicken as well. Rub the chicken – inside and out – with salt, and the outside with a little paprika as well. Brush a little melted butter over the chicken and roast it at Gas Mark 6 (400°F) until it is just tender. I prefer to do this in a covered roasting tin, or, if this is not possible, I cover the chicken with foil. Take out the chicken and put it on a rack over a baking dish and return it to the oven, breast side down for 5 minutes, then breast side up for another 5 minutes, basting it with an extra knob of butter or a little fat from the tin until nicely browned and crisp.

While the chicken is browning, pour off all the fat from the roasting tin – don't throw it away, it is marvellous for brushing over chops before grilling. Put the roasting tin with all the residue over a low flame, add the chicken stock, a handful of chopped tarragon and a good dash of brandy and turn up the heat. Cook until the liquid has been reduced to about half. Add the cream and simmer gently over a low flame until the sauce has thickened. Do not carve the chicken but cut it into convenient pieces with poultry shears or kitchen scissors, and serve the sauce separately.

Roast duck

My method of roasting duck may sound slightly unusual and it does require quite a bit of attention, but it is attention well spent – the end result will be crackling that is really crisp and meat that is beautifully moist and full of flavour.

1 duck   1 glassful red wine
salt, pepper, paprika

Clean the duck well – I use eyebrow tweezers to deal with stubborn stubbles. Wash the duck, wipe it dry, but do not truss it. Rub the duck, inside and out, with salt, pepper and paprika. As you do this, press down where the fat is thickest – particularly at the leg joints – and pay special attention to the bit of skin which overlaps at the neck opening. Remove any loose bits of fat – these make lovely dripping when rendered down. Leave the duck in a cool place for as long as possible – overnight if you can.

Put the duck into a roasting tin, breast side down and add a glass of red wine. Cover the tin with a lid and put it into the oven at Gas Mark 3 (325°F). After about 15 minutes the skin should be slightly transparent.

Now prick the skin all over with a thin-pronged fork, being careful not to go further than the skin and fat. Turn the duck on its back, replace the lid and put the duck back into the oven until it is tender. For a medium-sized duck this should take about 45–50 minutes, but much depends on the distribution of the meat and the proportion of fat. During this time gently prick the skin from time to time and if necessary, press down on the skin where the fat is thickest with the back of a fork to make the fat run.

When the duck is tender, turn up the oven heat to maximum and place the duck on a rack over a roasting tin or the lid of the tin in which it was roasted (the fat which will have collected in the baking tin makes superb dripping and the juices underneath, once the fat has been removed, very good basis for soups or sauces). Have a good look at the skin and prick it once more where the fat is thickest. Now roast the duck – without lid of course – breast side down for about 5 minutes at top heat, then turn it over and complete roasting, breast side upwards for another 5–10 minutes until the skin is very crisp and brown. The exact timing depends on how quickly your oven will heat up to top heat and you will simply have to watch it. I do not carve the duck in the traditional way, but simply cut it into convenient pieces with poultry shears or sharp kitchen scissors. It tastes better that way – just try it!

And I am all against anything which could possibly spoil the crispness of the skin – such as decorating the duck with slices of orange or whatever. The orange slices on the cover of this book are due to 'artistic licence' by the photographer!

Vegetables

I wish someone would tell me how to harvest young tender peas without eating at least half the crop while picking them. Or scrape carrots without nibbling – how to prepare a cauliflower and not pinch a few sprigs and slice a kohlrabi and find all the slices still intact afterwards, not half the slices because I have munched my way through the rest . . .

Probably it all dates back to my childhood when 'pinching while picking' was the order of the day and we grew far more vegetables than the family could ever consume: fat stalks of asparagus and small, sweet Brussels sprouts, barely larger than a pea, to be eaten with brown breadcrumbs sizzling in butter; dill growing in abundance, waist high like weeds; green peppers sown between rows of tomatoes to give them extra flavour . . .

All this abundance also left me with the right respect for vegetables – to cook them as soon as they were harvested, to treat them gently and use them to the last scrap – even to making soup out of the pea pods. There were other dishes too that I treasure to this day – peas cooked with lettuce leaves and butter, marrow with cream and fresh dill, and a surplus of mushrooms transformed into a Hungarian gulyas – plus a whole host of others . . .

Autumn vegetable casserole

4 oz (100g) bacon
2 tablespoons olive oil
2 large thinly sliced onions
1–2 crushed cloves garlic
1 red pepper
1 green pepper
1 yellow pepper
2–3 medium-sized potatoes
   or 6–8 small potatoes
salt and pepper

a sprig of rosemary
chopped marjoram and basil
1–2 handfuls diced white
   cabbage
1 handful shelled peas
5–6 small carrots
4 unpeeled and diced
   courgettes
grated Parmesan cheese

Dice the bacon and keep the lean pieces on one side. Heat the olive oil in a thick casserole, add the fat bits of bacon first and cook over gentle heat for the fat to seep out. Add the sliced onion and the lean bacon and brown everything together lightly. Add the crushed garlic as well and stir, then add the deseeded peppers cut into strips or squares and the potatoes. (If using small potatoes, just scrub them and add with their skins.) Season with salt and pepper, add the herbs and simmer in a covered casserole for about 10 minutes, then add the chopped cabbage, the peas, carrots and courgettes. Leave to simmer very gently – in a covered casserole – until the vegetables are just tender. Additional liquid should not be necessary, but occasional stirring is required. Adjust the seasoning if needed and serve with plenty of grated Parmesan cheese.

Cauliflower-in-a-bonnet

1 cauliflower	1 tablespoon flour
2½ oz (70g) butter	5 fl oz (140ml) sour cream
3 eggs	salt
2 tablespoons grated Parmesan cheese	butter and flour for the dish

Cook the cauliflower in boiling salted water – or steam it – until just tender. Drain. Separate the egg yolks and whites. Cream the butter until fluffy, then beat in the egg yolks one by one. Gradually beat in the Parmesan cheese, the flour and then the sour cream by the spoonful. Whisk the egg whites with a pinch of salt until stiff and fold into the mixture. Spread about a quarter of this mixture over the bottom of a buttered and floured gratin or pie dish, set the drained cauliflower on top and mask completely with the remaining mixture. Bake at Gas Mark 5 (375°F) until nicely browned on top – about 15–20 minutes.

Celeriac fritters

1 large celeriac	1–2 lightly beaten eggs
salt	fine breadcrumbs
1 large onion	1 tablespoon grated Parmesan cheese
1–2 tablespoons oil	
seasoned flour	oil for frying

Wash and peel the celeriac and cut it into slices about ⅓ inch thick. Sprinkle with salt. Chop the onion finely and simmer it

gently in the hot oil until softened and barely coloured. Add
the celeriac slices and a dash of water. Cover with a lid and
simmer very gently until the celeriac is tender, shaking the pan
from time to time. Leave to cool in the pan. Lift out the slices
very carefully so that some of the onion purée will cling to
each slice, and turn the slices first in seasoned flour, then in
lightly beaten egg and finally in fine breadcrumbs to which the
Parmesan has been added. Fry the slices – not too many at the
same time – in hot oil which should be just deep enough for
the slices to 'float'. Drain on kitchen paper and serve while still
hot.

Celeriac Florentine

1 celeriac
a little clear stock
a little lemon juice
1 lump sugar
1 finely chopped small onion
a little butter
½ lb (225g) deep-frozen
  spinach
salt and pepper

grated nutmeg
4 oz (120g) chopped ham
1 heaped tablespoon butter
1 flat tablespoon flour
9 fl oz (250ml) milk
grated Parmesan cheese
2 egg yolks, lightly beaten
breadcrumbs and butter
  for the top

Wash and peel the celeriac and cut it into slices. Put the slices
into a saucepan and just cover them with stock to which a little
lemon juice and a lump of sugar have been added. Simmer
gently until the celeriac is tender and practically all the liquid
has been absorbed. Chop the onion, simmer it gently in a little
butter and add the spinach. Cover with a lid and leave to cook.
Season with salt, pepper and a little nutmeg. Put the cooked

spinach in a buttered gratin dish and cover with the celeriac slices. Sprinkle the chopped ham over the top.

Melt the tablespoon of butter in a saucepan, stir in the flour and blend in the milk. Cook until the sauce has thickened. Season with salt, pepper and a little nutmeg and stir in a good tablespoon Parmesan cheese and the lightly beaten egg yolks. Pour over the celeriac and ham, sprinkle with breadcrumbs and grated Parmesan cheese and dot with butter. Brown in the oven or under a hot grill.

Courgette fritters

1 lb (450g) firm courgettes	flour
salt	oil for frying
2 eggs	
3½ oz (100g) grated	
Parmesan cheese	

Wipe the courgettes, then cut them into slices and sprinkle with salt. Cover and leave for ½ hour.

Make a batter with the eggs, salt and Parmesan cheese.

Drain the courgettes. Pat dry the slices with kitchen paper. Dip the slices first into flour, then into the batter and fry in plenty of hot oil. Drain on kitchen paper and serve at once.

Courgettes with tomatoes and bacon

1 lb (450g) courgettes
4 oz (100g) bacon
1 small onion
1–2 tablespoons olive oil
3 skinned, chopped tomatoes

salt and pepper
pinch of sugar
finely chopped basil and
   marjoram

Wipe over the courgettes – unless they are rather muddy in which case they will have to be washed as well. Cut the courgettes into dice, no need to peel them. Dice the bacon. Finely chop the onion. Heat the olive oil in a thick saucepan. Add first the fat bits of bacon and when the fat begins to run, add the onion, the remaining bacon and the diced courgettes. Brown all together lightly for about 5 minutes. Add the skinned and chopped tomatoes, salt, pepper, a pinch of sugar and the finely chopped herbs. Cover and leave to simmer until the courgettes are tender.

Creamed Jerusalem artichokes

1½ lb (675g) Jerusalem
   artichokes
dash of wine vinegar or a
   slice of lemon
2 tablespoons butter

salt and pepper
3–4 fl oz (85–110ml) good
   stock
3–4 fl oz (85–110ml) cream
chopped parsley

Wash and scrape the artichokes and throw them into a bowl of cold water to which a slice of lemon or a dash of wine vinegar has been added to stop discoloration. Slice the artichokes.

Melt the butter in a fairly wide saucepan, add the well-drained artichokes (pat them dry lightly with kitchen towelling). Cook the artichokes gently in the butter, having covered the saucepan with a lid, shaking the pan from time to time. Add salt, pepper and the stock. Simmer until the artichokes are tender – this varies according to their age and size, but it can be as little as 8–10 minutes, and on no account should they be allowed to overcook. By this time most of the liquid will have been absorbed. Now add the cream and mix very gently. Reheat and serve sprinkled with plenty of freshly chopped parsley.

Fennel au gratin

2 large fennel bulbs
9 fl oz (250ml) cream
salt
grated nutmeg
1 tablespoon chopped
  parsley

2 tablespoons grated cheese
1 heaped tablespoon
  breadcrumbs
a few flakes butter

Clean the fennel and cook the bulbs in boiling salted water until just tender. Slice the cooked fennel and arrange the slices in layers in a buttered gratin dish. (Fennel varies in size, but there should be enough to fill a gratin dish to within about 1 inch from the top.) Season the cream with salt and a little nutmeg and mix in the chopped parsley and a tablespoon of the grated cheese. Pour over the fennel, sprinkle breadcrumbs and the remaining grated cheese over the top. Dot with a few flakes of butter and bake at Gas Mark 6 (400°F) until brown and crisp on top.

Lecso

Delicious in its own right, it could be called a 'Hungarian cousin' of ratatouille. Spiced sausage cut into small pieces can be used instead of the bacon, and sometimes a lightly beaten egg per person is stirred in at the end of the cooking time and allowed to set.

1 lb (450g) green peppers
1 lb (450g) ripe tomatoes
4 oz (110g) bacon
2 tablespoons good dripping
  or olive oil

1 large onion, sliced
paprika
salt

Halve the green peppers, remove their seeds and stems and then cut the peppers into fairly wide strips. Scald the tomatoes, then dip them into cold water, skin and quarter them. Chop the bacon fairly coarsely. Heat the dripping – or olive oil – in a thick pan, add the bacon and fry lightly until transparent. Add the sliced onion and continued frying until bacon and onion are lightly browned. Add the paprika, stir and then add the green peppers and the tomatoes. Simmer gently until the green peppers are soft, then add salt to taste.

Marrow with cream and fresh dill

1 medium-sized marrow
salt
2 tablespoons butter
1 small, finely chopped onion
  or shallot
2 scant tablespoons flour

about 1 ladleful clear stock
1 tablespoon chopped
  parsley
1 heaped tablespoon finely
  chopped fresh dill
5 fl oz (140ml) sour cream

Peel and quarter the marrow, remove the seeds. Shred or grate the marrow, using a fairly coarse grater. Sprinkle with salt, cover and leave for about ¾ hour. Melt the butter in a saucepan, add the chopped onion and allow this to soften in the butter. Stir in the flour and gradually add the stock to give a fairly thick sauce. Squeeze out all the moisture from the marrow, add the marrow, parsley and dill. Stir in the cream and leave to simmer until the marrow is tender – about half an hour. Adjust seasoning if necessary – there should be a definite sweet/sour flavour and you may have to add a dash of wine vinegar. Incidentally, if you cannot get fresh dill, use a little of the liquid from pickled cucumber – it usually contains fresh dill.

Mushroom gulyas

1 heaped tablespoon butter
   or good dripping
1 large onion, chopped
1 lb (450g) cleaned, sliced
   mushrooms
1 lightly heaped dessertspoon
   paprika

salt
1 teaspoon caraway seeds
1 tablespoon tomato purée
1 teaspoon flour
5 fl oz (140ml) sour cream

Heat the butter or dripping in a thick saucepan, add the chopped onion and allow it to soften. Turn up the heat and add the mushrooms and fry lightly until onion and mushrooms are lightly browned and the resulting liquid has almost evaporated. Dust with paprika, stir and add a dash of water. Also add salt, caraway seeds and tomato purée. Simmer until the mushrooms are tender. Additional liquid should not be necessary, but watch it and stir from time to time. Mix the flour with the sour cream, add to the mushrooms and simmer for another 5 minutes and serve.

Peas cooked with lettuce

Quantities do not really matter – it is the method which counts!

Rinse but do not dry a fairly thick saucepan. Wash the outer leaves of a lettuce – do not dry them – and use some of these to line the bottom of the saucepan. Shell and rinse as many peas as you will need. If there are a few very thin pea pods with barely any peas in them, do not try to prise them open, just remove the string as for French beans and add them as well. Wash and quarter the lettuce heart and put this on top of the peas, together with a few spring onions, salt, pepper and some very generous dots of butter. Cover with the remaining lettuce leaves and dot with a little more butter. Cover the saucepan with a lid and simmer very gently until the peas are tender – this obviously depends on their size and their age, but no extra liquid should be required. That is all – except that if I am uncertain as to the age of the peas I add a small pinch of sugar with the rest of the seasoning. I prefer the peas in their natural liquid, but if you like a slightly thicker sauce, simply work a teaspoon of butter into a teaspoon of flour and add this to the peas towards the end of the cooking time.

Summer vegetable pudding

1 lightly heaped plateful of
    summer vegetables –
young carrots, peas, beans,
cauliflower, some celery
stalks – all diced or sliced
except, of course, for the
peas and the cauliflower,
which should be broken
into small rosettes
salt and pepper

butter and flour for the
    pudding basin
3 eggs
1 heaped tablespoon butter
1 scant tablespoon flour
9 fl oz (250ml) milk
grated nutmeg
1 heaped tablespoon grated
    cheese
melted butter

Cook the vegetables in boiling salted water until just tender –
they should still have some 'bite' to them. Drain – keep the
water for stock – and dust them lightly with salt and a little
pepper.

Butter and flour a pudding basin. Separate the egg yolks and
whites. Melt the butter in a saucepan, stir in the flour and
gradually add the milk. Cook over gentle heat until the sauce
has thickened. Add salt, pepper and a little grated nutmeg. Stir
in the cheese. Remove from heat and beat in the egg yolks –
one by one – and add the vegetables. Whisk the egg whites
until stiff and fold into the mixture. Pile into the pudding basin
and steam for about 1 hour. Turn out the pudding on to a
heated serving dish and either pour a little melted butter over
it or hand it separately.

Tomatoes cooked with white cabbage

2 lb (900g) firm white
  cabbage
1 lb (450g) ripe tomatoes
2 tablespoons butter or
  rendered bacon fat
1 large onion, sliced or diced

1 heaped teaspoon sugar
salt
dash of wine vinegar
a little cream (about 2
  tablespoons)

Shred the cabbage finely. Skin and quarter the tomatoes. Heat the butter in a large pan, add the onion and allow to soften in the butter. Sprinkle with sugar, turn up the heat and stir until the sugar has caramelized. Add the shredded cabbage and the quartered tomatoes – stand aside a little since the fat is apt to spatter – and leave to simmer over low heat until the cabbage is tender and the tomatoes have practically melted. Add salt and a dash of vinegar. Stir, then add about two tablespoons cream. Reheat gently and serve.

White cabbage baked with bacon

1 firm white cabbage, about
  1 lb (450g)
1 teaspoon salt
1 heaped tablespoon butter
  for the dish

6 oz (170g) streaky bacon
  rashers
6 tablespoons (150ml) good
  beef consommé

Remove the outer leaves from the cabbage. Make a few incisions in the stalk and, if necessary, remove any 'woody' parts. Bring a large pan of water to the boil, add the salt and the cabbage and cook it until the stem is barely tender. Drain well. (Alternatively, steam the cabbage over a large pan of salted water until just tender.)

Butter a soufflé dish and preheat the oven to Gas Mark 4 (350°F). Trim the rinds off the bacon rashers. Set the drained cabbage in the buttered dish and pour the consommé over it. Cover with overlapping slices of bacon. Bake until the bacon is nicely crisped. Serve the cabbage cut into wedges, each slice topped with some of the bacon and a little of the hot consommé poured over it.

Potatoes

I love potatoes – big baked ones, all nice and fluffy with a large dollop of butter in the centre, or small waxy ones cradled in a light mustard dressing; hot potato dishes to serve with cold meat, and little potato ramekins perfect for supper on a tray by the fireside.

I would love to emulate Francatelli, chef to Queen Victoria, who wrote a whole book about potato dishes, but here is a selection of my own favourites.

Baked potato supper

Small potatoes simply scrubbed, halved and baked with a sprinkling of coarse salt and caraway seeds are lovely for eating round a fire. Sometimes I slip in just a knob of butter or some easily melting cheese, but for a more substantial supper dish try the following with its unusual combination of hot and cold.

THE SUNDAY EXPRESS COOKBOOK

2 lb (900g) small or medium-sized potatoes
1 tablespoon coarse salt
2 tablespoons caraway seeds
butter
½ lb (225g) sieved cottage cheese

about 4 fl oz (110ml) cream
1 finely grated shallot
1 heaped tablespoon each finely chopped parsley and watercress
salt and white pepper

Scrub the potatoes but do not scrape them. Mix together the salt and caraway seeds (quantities may have to be increased according to the cut surface of the potatoes, but the ratio should be 1 tablespoon salt to 2 tablespoons caraway seeds) and sprinkle over a flat plate. Halve the potatoes lengthways and dip the cut side into the mixture. Arrange the potatoes – cut side uppermost – on a lightly buttered baking sheet and dot each potato with a small flake of butter. Bake at Gas Mark 6 (400°F) until they are nicely puffed up and browned on top. The time varies according to type and size of potato, but count on about 30–45 minutes.

Meanwhile mix together the sieved cottage cheese and the cream – add just enough to give a thick creamy consistency. Beat in the grated shallot, parsley and watercress, and season with salt and white pepper. Chill the mixture, then pile it in the centre of a serving dish and serve with the piping hot potatoes.

Caraway potatoes with sour cream

1 lb (450g) medium-sized potatoes
butter for the dish
salt

1 heaped teaspoon caraway seeds
8–10 fl oz (225–275ml) sour cream

98

Peel the potatoes and cut them into fairly thin slices. Put the slices into a colander and rinse them under a warm tap – this will get rid of excess starch. Pat the sliced potatoes dry on kitchen paper.

Butter a gratin dish well and put the potatoes into the dish. Sprinkle with salt and caraway seeds and mix lightly so that the salt and caraway seeds are evenly distributed. Bake at Gas Mark 5 (375°F) for about 50 minutes – until the potatoes are cooked and nicely browned. No butter is needed, but turn the potato slices over carefully from time to time while they are baking so that they brown evenly.

When the potatoes are browned, stir in the sour cream – the quantity depends on how thinly you have cut the potatoes. Stir carefully and serve at once – there is no need to put the dish back into the oven to heat it through.

Crisp and creamy potato supper

1 lb (450g) waxy potatoes
6 hardboiled eggs
¼–½ lb (115–225g) spiced
  sausage
10 fl oz (275ml) sour cream

2 eggs
salt and pepper
pinch of nutmeg
a little butter

The choice of sausages is a matter of taste – I prefer the rather highly spiced Spanish sausages, which I slice fairly thinly. Lightly fried bacon can also be used for this recipe and it tastes pretty good too when made with well-spiced cooked pork sausages.

Boil the potatoes in their skins. Peel and slice them while they are still hot. Slice the hardboiled eggs and the sausage. (If using bacon, dice it before frying it lightly.) Butter a gratin dish. Arrange the potatoes, hardboiled eggs and sausage in the dish – not in layers, just mix them lightly. Stir the eggs into the sour cream, season with salt, pepper and a pinch of nutmeg. Pour over the potatoes in the dish. Dot with a few flakes of butter and set it in a hot oven (Gas Mark 6, 400°F) until the top is nicely crisped and brown. Serve with a fresh green salad.

Herbed potatoes

1½ lb (650g) cooked, peeled potatoes
2 oz (60g) butter
1½ oz (40g) flour
1 pint (575ml) good beef stock

1 heaped tablespoon finely chopped fresh marjoram
salt and pepper

Best cooked in a flameproof dish from which it can also be served.

Slice the potatoes to about the thickness of a 10p piece. Melt the butter over low heat, blend in the flour and gradually stir in the stock. Add the marjoram. Leave to simmer very gently for about 5 minutes, then add the potatoes. Leave to simmer over low heat until the potatoes are warmed through. Taste and if necessary add a little salt and pepper. That's all – except for possibly a small dash of cream added just before serving.

Mustard potatoes

1 lb (450g) small, waxy
  potatoes
salt and pepper
2 egg yolks
dash of white wine vinegar

1 heaped tablespoon Dijon
  mustard
4 tablespoons olive oil
finely chopped chives

Boil the potatoes in their skins, then peel and slice them into a bowl while they are still hot – unless you have managed to get very small potatoes of roughly the same size, in which case leave them whole. Sprinkle with salt.

Put the egg yolks into a small bowl, add a pinch each of salt and pepper, a dash of wine vinegar and a heaped tablespoon of Dijon mustard. Stand the bowl over steam and gradually add the olive oil. Stir over steam, making sure that the water underneath does not boil or touch the bowl until thickened, which will happen almost instantly. Pour over the potatoes and mix very lightly. Cover and leave for about 5–10 minutes. Sprinkle with finely chopped chives before serving.

Potato gulyas

2 lb (900g) waxy potatoes
½ lb (225g) onions
1 tablespoon lard or oil
1 heaped tablespoon paprika
dash of wine vinegar
8 fl oz (225ml) clear stock
salt and pepper
1 teaspoon caraway seeds
1 teaspoon finely chopped
  marjoram

1 tablespoon concentrated
  tomato purée
1 teaspoon flour

Optional additions:
  5 fl oz (140ml) cream or
  sour cream
  4 pairs Frankfurter
  sausages

101

Peel the potatoes and cut them into slices a bit thicker than a 10p piece. Put them into a large bowl and cover them with cold water. Chop the onions finely and soften them gently over low heat in lard or oil. When the onions are soft and slightly transparent, turn up the heat and stir until they are a nice golden brown, then stir in the paprika. Let it froth up, then add a dash of good wine vinegar. Pour in the stock and stir again. Rinse the potatoes under a cold tap, shake off the surplus water and add them to the onions, together with salt, pepper, caraway seeds and marjoram. Also add the tomato purée and stir. Cover and leave to simmer over a low flame until the potatoes are soft and just beginning to fall apart. If you feel in an extravagant mood, thicken with cream or sour cream, alternatively slake the flour with a little cold water, stir into the potatoes and leave to simmer until thickened. Slice the Frankfurter sausages into the gulyas and heat gently before serving.

Potato ramekins
(serves 2)

Use either one smallish ramekin per person or a larger gratin dish – say one measuring 6 by 6 inches or its round equivalent.

butter for the dish	powdered marjoram
½ lb (225g) potatoes	3–4 fl oz (85–100ml) stock
oil or butter for frying	5 fl oz (140ml) cream or sour
salt and pepper	cream
paprika	2 eggs
powdered rosemary	nutmeg and mace

Butter the gratin dish or the ramekins. Peel and slice the potatoes and fry the slices lightly on both sides in butter or oil.

102

Lift out the slices with a slotted spoon and dust them with salt, pepper, paprika, powdered rosemary and marjoram. Arrange the potatoes in the dish (or dishes) and moisten with good clear stock – it should just about cover the potatoes. Cover with foil and put the dish into the oven at Gas Mark 5 (375°F) until the potatoes are just soft – about 30 minutes – by which time most of the liquid will have been absorbed. Whisk together the cream – or sour cream – eggs, mace and nutmeg and if there is any liquid left in the dish whisk this in as well. Pour over the potatoes and return the dish to the oven – uncovered – at Gas Mark 7 (425°F) until it is all puffed up and the top has browned nicely. Serve at once.

Potatoes in sour cream

1½ lb (675g) waxy potatoes
1 medium onion
1½ oz (40g) butter

10 fl oz (280ml) sour cream
salt and pepper
chopped chives

Boil the potatoes in their skins, peel while still hot, and cut into slices. Chop or slice the onion finely. Melt the butter, add the onion and allow it to soften. Add the sour cream, stir and then add the sliced potatoes. Simmer gently until the potatoes are heated through. Season with salt and pepper and serve sprinkled with plenty of chopped chives.

Swiss potatoes

2 lb (900g) waxy potatoes
5 oz (125g) Emmenthal
  cheese
2 oz (50g) butter
1 heaped tablespoon flour
8 fl oz (225ml) milk

2 eggs
salt and pepper
grated nutmeg
4 fl oz (125ml) cream
butter, grated cheese and
  breadcrumbs for the top

Boil the potatoes in their skins and peel and slice them while they are still hot. Dice the Emmenthal cheese. Melt the butter in a saucepan, stir in the flour and gradually add the milk. Allow to cook gently until you have a fairly thick sauce. Separate the egg yolks and whites, then season the sauce with salt, pepper and a little grated nutmeg. Add the cream and then stir in the egg yolks, one by one and away from the heat. Add the diced cheese. Fold in the sliced potatoes. Whisk the egg whites until stiff and fold in these as well.

Butter a gratin dish and dust it lightly with breadcrumbs. Arrange the potato mixture in the dish and sprinkle the top with breadcrumbs and a little grated cheese. Pour a little melted butter over the top and bake at Gas Mark (375°F) until nicely browned on top – about 40 minutes.

Parmesan potatoes

Delicious as an accompaniment to roast meat, but also a splendid little supper dish in its own right if served with a fresh green salad. The only trouble is that it is almost impossible to give exact quantities.

Just butter a gratin dish and cover it with a layer of sliced, cooked potatoes. (Let the potatoes get cold before slicing.) Dot with a few flakes butter and sprinkle with grated Parmesan cheese. Moisten with sour cream. Then add another layer of cooked potatoes, dot with butter, sprinkle with grated Parmesan cheese and moisten with sour cream, and continue in this way until the dish is full – unless you are making it for only two people in which case stop when you want – or use a smaller dish. Bake at Gas Mark 4 (350°F) until nicely browned on top.

Supper dishes –
or hot starters

Intended primarily as hot supper dishes, practically all of these will make splendid hot starters for a dinner party. Some are very light and simple, like the baked eggs with sour cream; others, though very simple to prepare, are pretty sensational, like the cheese puffs which are really small individual soufflés baked in a scooped-out roll. Or the mushroom pudding which is like a soft, downy cloud scented with mushrooms.

There are also small delicacies like the mushrooms in a lemon sauce, or my favourite soufflé which I still prefer above all others. It is the blend of cheese with smoked oysters which I find so irresistible – but try for yourself . . .

Baked eggs with sour cream
(serves 4)

butter for the dish
5 eggs
1 tablespoon flour
5 fl oz (140ml) sour cream

salt
2 tablespoons Parmesan
    cheese
flakes of butter

Butter a gratin dish. Preheat the oven to Gas Mark 6 (400°F). Separate the yolk and white of one of the eggs. Whisk together the egg yolk, flour and sour cream with a pinch of salt. Whisk the egg white until stiff, then fold into the mixture. Spread half of this mixture into the gratin dish, dust with Parmesan cheese, then break the four eggs on top of this so that they sit side by side in the dish. Pile the remaining mixture over the top and sprinkle with more Parmesan cheese. Dot with a few flakes of softened butter and bake until nicely browned on top. Serve at once. Individual ramekin dishes can of course be used instead of one gratin dish.

Creamed eggs
(serves 4)

4 hardboiled eggs
butter for the dish
1 heaped tablespoon butter
1 lightly heaped tablespoon
  flour
¾ pint (425ml) milk

salt and pepper
pinch of mace
3 lightly heaped tablespoons
  Parmesan cheese
2–3 tablespoons cream
a few flakes of butter

Shell the eggs and halve them. Lightly butter a gratin dish. Preheat the oven to Gas Mark 7 (425°F).

Melt the butter in a saucepan, stir in the flour and cook gently until well blended. Gradually add the milk and seasoning, stirring all the time over a low flame until the mixture is very thick. Stir in 2 tablespoons of the Parmesan cheese and the cream. Chop the egg whites finely – keep the yolks on one side. Pour about a third of the sauce into the gratin dish, sprinkle with the chopped egg whites, cover with another layer of sauce, then crumble the egg yolks over this and cover with the remaining sauce. (For a slightly more elegant – though more time-consuming – finish, sieve rather than crumble the egg yolks – it makes no difference to the taste, but the texture is slightly smoother.) Sprinkle with the remaining Parmesan cheese, dot with a few flakes of butter and put into the hot oven until nicely browned on top. Serve with crusty French bread and a fresh green salad.

Eggs in a cloud
(serves 4)

4 hardboiled eggs	3 tablespoons butter
1 heaped tablespoon butter	salt
1–2 scraped anchovies	pinch of mace
pinch of cayenne	2 tablespoons sour cream
2 tablespoons cream	1 teaspoon flour
2 eggs	

Preheat the oven to Gas Mark 7 (425°F). Butter a gratin dish.

Halve the hardboiled eggs and scoop out the yolks. Cream the tablespoon of butter and beat in the hardboiled eggs. Add the scraped anchovies, a pinch of cayenne and the cream (salt is not usually necessary since it is provided by the anchovies). Arrange mounds of this mixture in the centre of the halved egg whites and set them in the gratin dish.

Separate the yolks and whites of the eggs. Cream the butter until light and fluffy, beat in the egg yolks one by one, beating well after each addition. Season with salt and a little mace and beat in the sour cream. Whip the egg whites until stiff and fold into the mixture, together with the flour. Mask the eggs with this and put them into the hot oven until nicely browned on top. Serve at once.

Cheese puffs
(serves 4)

2 eggs
2 oz (60g) butter
1½ oz (40g) flour
¼ pint (140ml) milk
2½ oz (70g) grated Cheddar
  or Cheshire cheese

salt and pepper
pinch of powdered mace
4 crusty rolls
butter for the rolls

Preheat the oven to Gas Mark 7 (425°F). Separate the egg yolks and whites. Melt the 2 oz butter in a saucepan, stir in the flour. Gradually add the milk and cook until the sauce has thickened. Add cheese, salt, pepper and mace. Remove from the heat and beat in the egg yolks, one by one. Set aside to cool.

While the sauce is cooling, halve the rolls and scoop out all the crumb – use it for breadcrumbs later on. Prick the resulting shells lightly with a fork, spread the insides with butter and set them on a baking sheet. Put the shells into the oven for a minute or two – the insides should just be tinged with colour.

Whisk the egg whites until stiff and fold into the cheese sauce. Pile the mixture into the shells and put them back into the oven for about 5–6 minutes. They will look rather spectacular – and they will taste every bit as good as they look – moist and still slightly runny inside, with the crisp shells making a perfect contrast.

Cheese ring

butter and flour for the dish
3 eggs
2 oz (60g) butter
pinch of salt
¼ pint (140ml) cream
  or sour cream

1½ oz (40g) grated Parmesan
  cheese
2½ oz (70g) flour

Butter and flour a 2-pint ring mould. Preheat the oven to Gas
Mark 8 (425°F). Separate the egg yolks and whites. Cream the
butter with a pinch of salt until light and fluffy and then beat in
the egg yolks, one by one. Gradually whisk in the cream – or
sour cream. The consistency should be that of not too stiffly
whipped cream. Whisk the egg whites until stiff and fold into
the mixture, alternately with the flour and the grated Parmesan
cheese. Tip the mixture into the prepared ring mould and
stand it in a large baking dish filled with enough water to come
halfway up the sides of the mould. Put it into the oven for
about 25–30 minutes, when the top should be just lightly
coloured and the mixture fairly firm to the touch. Turn it out
carefully on to a warmed serving dish and serve at once – it
will subside slightly, but still remain rather moist inside. Serve
a fresh green salad with it – or, for a rather more substantial
dish – fill the centre of the ring with some crisply cooked
French or runner beans tossed with a knob of butter and a
tablespoon of finely chopped ham.

Cheese and tomato supper
(serves 4)

1 lb (450g) tomatoes
butter for the dish
salt
3 eggs

4 oz (100g) grated Parmesan
  cheese
finely chopped parsley
a little cream or sour cream

Halve the tomatoes and carefully remove the pulp – save it for adding to sauces and stews. Set the tomato shells side by side in a buttered gratin dish and dust the insides lightly with salt.

Whisk the eggs very lightly, add the cheese, chopped parsley, salt and a little cream or sour cream. Divide the mixture between the tomatoes and bake at Gas Mark 6 (400°F) until nicely browned on top.

Mushrooms in lemon sauce

¾ lb (350g) button
  mushrooms
1½ oz (40g) butter
juice of 1 lemon
5 fl oz (140ml) good clear
  consommé

3 egg yolks
salt
ground mace

Clean the mushrooms, but leave them whole. Melt the butter, add the mushrooms and immediately squeeze the lemon juice over them. Cover the pan and leave the mushrooms to simmer very gently until just tender, shaking the pan from time to time. Remove even the slightest trace of fat from the consommé.

Whisk together the egg yolks, consommé and seasonings, then drain the liquid from the mushrooms and add to the mixture. Arrange the mushrooms in a pretty heatproof dish, pour the egg mixture over them and either set the dish over steam or put it in a large baking dish with hot water in the oven at Gas Mark 6 (400°F) until the sauce has set. Serve with lots of crusty French bread.

Hot mushroom savouries

1 shallot	1 level tablespoon flour
1 tablespoon butter	5 fl oz (140ml) milk
½ lb (225g) button	1 egg yolk
mushrooms, sliced	2 tablespoons Parmesan
chopped parsley	cheese
lemon juice	nutmeg
salt and pepper	slices of buttered bread
1 heaped tablespoon butter	Parmesan cheese for the top

Chop the shallot finely. Melt the tablespoon of butter, add the shallot and allow to soften. Add the sliced mushrooms, a little parsley and lemon juice and simmer gently until the mushrooms are cooked. Season with salt and pepper.

Melt the heaped tablespoon of butter in a thick saucepan, stir in the flour and gradually add the milk. Cook to a fairly thick sauce, then stir in the egg yolk – away from the heat – and the cooked mushrooms. Add the Parmesan cheese, taste and adjust the seasoning if necessary, adding a little nutmeg. Leave to get cold.

Cut the crusts off the buttered bread and cut the bread into squares. Spread the bread squares fairly thickly with the mushroom mixture and set them on a lightly buttered baking sheet. Sprinkle grated Parmesan cheese over the top and put into a hot oven – Gas Mark 7 (425°F) – until heated through.

Mushroom pudding
(serves 4)

butter and flour for the
   pudding basin
6 oz (170g) button
   mushrooms or 1 small
   packet (½ oz/15g) dried
   mushrooms
1 heaped tablespoon butter
1 tablespoon chopped
   parsley

salt and pepper
2 oz (60g) butter
2½ oz (70g) flour
4½ fl oz (130ml) milk
nutmeg
3 eggs

Button mushrooms are excellent for this, but dried continental boletus (porcini in Italian) are even better. Butter and flour a 2-pint pudding basin. Clean and slice the mushrooms. Melt the butter in a saucepan, add the sliced mushrooms and the chopped parsley and simmer gently until the mushrooms are cooked. Season with salt and pepper and leave to cool.

If you are using dried mushrooms, tip them into a small sieve and rinse them under a barely warm tap to get rid of any sand or grit, then put them into a small bowl and just cover them with warm water to soften them. (The water can be used for soups and stews, but strain it first.) After this, use as described for fresh mushrooms.

Melt the 2 oz butter in a saucepan, stir in the flour and gradually add the milk, nutmeg and salt and pepper. Cook until well thickened and the mixture leaves the sides of the saucepan clean. Remove from the heat and allow to cool a little. Separate the egg yolks and whites. Beat the egg yolks – one by one – into the butter and flour mixture. Whisk the egg whites until stiff. Fold the whites into the yolks mixture, then fold in the cooked and cooled mushrooms. Pile the mixture into the prepared pudding basin and put it over steam. Do not cover the pudding basin – just the top of the steamer – but make sure that there is plenty of space between the top of the pudding basin and the top of the steamer, as the pudding will rise quite a bit. If necessary, make a sort of dome with kitchen foil instead of using the steamer lid to give the necessary height for the pudding to expand. Steam for about 45 minutes. Turn out carefully on to a heated dish and serve at once – it will collapse like a soufflé if left for any length of time.

Mushroom and cheese soufflé
(serves 4)

1 small onion	butter and flour for the dish
2 oz (60g) butter	1 heaped tablespoon butter
½ lb (225g) button mushrooms	1 flat tablespoon flour
salt and pepper	5 fl oz (140ml) milk
1 heaped teaspoon flour	2 eggs
2 tablespoons cream	2 tablespoons grated Parmesan cheese

Chop the onion finely. Melt the 2 oz butter and soften the chopped onion in this without browning. Clean, wipe and thinly slice the mushrooms. Add them to the onion, cover and leave to simmer until the mushrooms are cooked. Add salt and pepper to taste. Slake the teaspoon of flour with the cream and stir into the mushroom mixture. Leave to simmer until lightly thickened, then put the mixture either into a buttered and floured soufflé dish or divide it between several small ramekin dishes.

Preheat the oven to Gas Mark 6 (400°F). Melt the tablespoon of butter in a thick saucepan, add the flour and stir. Gradually add the milk, salt and pepper and cook over gentle heat until thickened. Separate the egg yolks and whites. Stir the yolks into the butter and flour mixture. Finally fold in the grated Parmesan cheese. Top the mushrooms with the cheese mixture and put the dish (or dishes) into the hot oven until nicely puffed up and browned (about 20 minutes if using a soufflé dish – a matter of minutes if using individual ramekin dishes).

My favourite soufflé

a small tin smoked oysters
butter and flour for the dish
1½ oz (40g) butter
1 oz (25g) flour
½ pint (275ml) milk
4 oz (115g) grated cheese
    (Cheddar, Cheshire or
    Caerphilly)

salt and pepper
ground mace
4 eggs

Preheat the oven to Gas Mark 6 (400°F). Butter and flour a 2-pint soufflé dish. Put the smoked oysters in the soufflé dish and moisten them with a little of their own juice.

Melt the butter in a thick saucepan, stir in the flour and gradually add the milk. Stir over a low flame until well thickened, then stir in the cheese and the seasonings. Cook very gently until well blended, then remove from the heat. Separate the egg yolks and whites. Cool the mixture a little and then beat in the egg yolks, one by one. Whisk the egg whites until stiff and fold into the mixture. Pile on top of the smoked oysters and bake until puffed up and golden brown – about 15–18 minutes.

Soft herring roes can be used instead of the smoked oysters, and tinned roes are excellent for this recipe – just drain them and fry them gently in a little butter first.

Spinach soufflés

The mixture could of course be used to make one large soufflé, but using small individual soufflé dishes is preferable on several counts: the actual baking time is much shorter – you can prepare the basic mixture in advance and just whisk the egg whites and slip the soufflés into the oven while your guests are sipping their drinks. And small individual soufflés – all nicely puffed up – look just that much more festive!

12–14 oz (340–390g) cooked
  spinach
salt
ground mace or nutmeg
1 heaped tablespoon butter
1 lightly heaped tablespoon
  flour

4 fl oz (110ml) milk
2 eggs
1 oz (25g) grated Parmesan
  cheese (optional)
butter and flour for the dishes

Make sure that all water has been drained from the spinach. Sieve the cooked spinach or pass it through a blender or food processor so that you have a fine purée of spinach. Season with salt and ground mace or nutmeg.

Melt the butter, stir in the flour and gradually add the milk. Cook to a thick sauce. Add the spinach and stir to blend.

116

Separate the egg yolks and whites. Beat the yolks into the spinach mixture and fold in the grated Parmesan (I have made this an 'optional' because the soufflé mixture is excellent even without it, but Parmesan adds a little more 'bite').

Preheat the oven to Gas Mark 6 (400°F). Whisk the egg whites until stiff and fold into the mixture. Divide between four or six buttered and floured small soufflé dishes (quantities are sufficient for four small soufflé dishes measuring 3 inches in diameter or six dishes measuring 2½ inches in diameter). Bake until nicely puffed up and just a little browned on top. Serve at once.

Cauliflower soufflé

1 large or 2 small cauliflowers	3 eggs
salt	salt, pepper, nutmeg
1 teaspoon sugar	2 oz (55g) grated Parmesan
1 heaped tablespoon butter	or Caerphilly cheese
1 lightly heaped tablepoon flour	flaked almonds
½ pint (275ml) milk	butter and flour for the soufflé dish

Trim the cauliflower and make a few incisions at the base of the stem. Put the cauliflower into cold salted water for 20–30 minutes.

Steam or cook the cauliflower in lightly salted water to which a teaspoon of sugar has been added. When just tender, drain and then divide into sprigs.

Preheat the oven to Gas Mark 5 (375°F). Butter and lightly flour a soufflé dish (or a deep gratin dish). Melt the butter in a thick saucepan, stir in the flour over low flame until well blended, then add the milk gradually and cook, stirring constantly, until the mixture is well thickened and leaves the sides of the saucepan clean. Separate the egg yolks and whites. Stir the egg yolks – one by one – into the slightly cooled mixture. Add salt, pepper and nutmeg. Whisk the egg whites until stiff and fold into the mixture alternately with the grated cheese. Finally fold in the cauliflower sprigs. Pile the mixture into the prepared dish and sprinkle with flaked almonds. Bake until well risen and browned on top. Serve at once.

Ham and cauliflower gratin

1 cauliflower
6–8 oz (170–225g) chopped
  ham
4 egg yolks
½ pint (275ml) sour cream

salt and pepper
breadcrumbs
grated Parmesan cheese
butter

Cook the cauliflower in boiling salted water or steam until it is just tender. Butter a gratin dish and divide the cauliflower carefully into small sprigs. Arrange alternate layers of cauliflower and chopped ham in the dish. Whisk together the egg yolks, sour cream, very little salt and a sprinkling of pepper and pour into the dish. Sprinkle with fine breadcrumbs and Parmesan cheese. Dot with small flakes of butter. Bake in a hot oven (Gas Mark 6/400°F) until nicely browned on top – about 10–15 minutes.

Risotto

1 heaped tablespoon bone
  marrow
1 heaped tablespoon butter
1 small onion, finely grated
½ lb (225g) risotto (Arborio)
  rice

1 pint (550ml) good chicken
  or veal stock
¼ lb (110g) grated Parmesan
  cheese
extra grated Parmesan cheese
  for serving

You will need about 1 pint liquid in all, but this varies a little according to the rice. Some of the stock may be replaced with white wine.

Put the bone marrow and the butter into a thick saucepan, and stir over low flame until melted. Add the grated onion and allow this to soften in the fat. Add the rice, previously rinsed under a hot tap and shaken dry. Stir over low heat until the rice is transparent and well coated with the fat, then add about ½ pint hot stock and leave to simmer, gradually adding more stock as this becomes necessary. Allow to simmer gently until the rice is just tender – about 20–25 minutes – then stir in the grated Parmesan cheese. For extra richness, also stir in a heaped tablespoon butter, but this is not strictly necessary. Serve with grated Parmesan cheese.

Ramekins

A particularly good dish for a fireside supper for two, though almost impossible to give exact quantities. I prefer to cook these in small individual dishes, but a slightly larger gratin dish can of course be used.

Simply butter two medium-sized ramekin dishes – or a small gratin dish. Cut some very thin slivers from a day-old French loaf and fry them in butter until golden brown and crisp. Pile the slices very loosely into the ramekins or the gratin dish – they should be about half full. Sprinkle with finely chopped lean ham or with small chunks of cooked gammon and cover with thin slivers of cheese – Gruyère for preference, but Cheddar or Caerphilly will do very nicely. Cover the top with some more thinly cut bread fried golden brown in butter. Whisk together ¾ cup milk with 3 eggs, salt, pepper and a little grated nutmeg and pour over the whole. Dot with small flakes of butter and stand the dish in a large roasting tin with water to come halfway up the gratin dish. Bake at Gas Mark 5 (375°F) until the egg mixture has set. Serve with a crisp green salad.

Spinach pudding

butter and flour for the
   pudding basin
1 lb (450g) spinach
2 rolls (at least 24 hours old)
a little milk
3½ oz (100g) butter
4 eggs
salt

nutmeg
1 tablespoon chopped
   parsley
3 fl oz (85ml) cream
1 oz (28g) fresh breadcrumbs
1 heaped tablespoon butter
1 heaped tablespoon fresh
   breadcrumbs

Butter and flour a pudding basin. Steam or cook the spinach in its own steam (i.e. in just the water clinging to the leaves after washing), shaking the pan from time to time and turning over the leaves frequently. Drain off all liquid, then put the spinach through the blender or food processor or sieve it. (1 lb raw spinach should result in approximately 7 oz cooked spinach.)

Grate the crust off the rolls and soak the crumb in a little milk to soften.

Cream the butter until light and fluffy. Separate the egg yolks and whites. Beat the yolks into the creamed butter, one by one, then add the sieved spinach, a little salt and grated nutmeg, the parsley and the cream. Squeeze out all moisture from the rolls and beat these in as well. Whisk the egg whites until stiff and fold into the mixture, alternately with the breadcrumbs. Arrange the mixture in the buttered and floured pudding basin and steam for about 1 hour.

Melt the heaped tablespoon of butter in a frying pan, stir in the heaped tablespoon of breadcrumbs and fry until they are golden brown and crisp.

Turn out the pudding on to a warmed serving dish and sprinkle with the fried breadcrumbs. Serve at once.

For a slightly more substantial dish surround the pudding with finely chopped ham and serve with a good, sharp tomato sauce.

Summer toasts

2 oz (50g) butter
1–2 finely scraped anchovies
5–6 slices bread
sliced tomatoes
thinly sliced cheese
2 large egg yolks

3 tablespoons flour
salt
grated nutmeg or mace
finely chopped parsley
1 tablespoon white wine

Preheat the oven to Gas Mark 6 (400°F). Cream the butter with the scraped anchovies and spread over the sliced bread. (I prefer brown bread, but it will taste very good with white bread too.) Set the bread side by side on a baking sheet. Cover

121

the bread with thinly sliced tomatoes and put thin slivers of cheese over the top. Cheddar or Cheshire are excellent, but I also like Caerphilly which I just crumble over the top. Whisk together the egg yolks with the flour, add a pinch each of salt and nutmeg (or mace), some chopped parsley and the white wine. Spread the mixture over the top of the tomatoes and the cheese and bake until nicely browned.

Supper shells

4 oz (110g) butter
1 shallot, finely grated
2 tablespoons flour
6 anchovies, finely scraped
1 cup chicken or veal stock
1 cup sour cream
3 egg yolks

salt and pepper
nutmeg
2 cups diced cooked chicken
breadcrumbs
grated Parmesan cheese
melted butter

Melt the butter and add the finely grated shallot. Allow to soften in the butter, then sprinkle in the flour and cook until the flour is lightly tinged with colour. Add the finely scraped anchovies and the stock. Stir until well blended, remove from heat and allow to cool. Add the sour cream and the egg yolks and season with very little salt (taste the mixture first because of the anchovies), pepper and a little grated nutmeg. Add the meat.

Butter some scallop shells and divide the mixture between them. Sprinkle with breadcrumbs and Parmesan cheese and pour a little melted butter over the top. Brown in the oven at Gas Mark 6 (400°F)

Salads, sauces
and accompaniments
– and some drinks

Avocado salad

3–4 heads of chicory
2 ripe avocado pears
a little lemon juice
1 green pepper, deseeded
  and cut into strips

2 tablespoons chopped
  walnuts
paprika

DRESSING
3 heaped tablespoons
  mayonnaise
1 tablespoon cream
dash of Worcestershire sauce
dash of tomato ketchup

salt and pepper
wine vinegar
French mustard
a little chopped fresh
  tarragon

Blend together all the ingredients for the dressing and taste. The best way to do this is to dip a small bit of chicory into the dressing. Adjust the seasoning if necessary.

Slice the chicory. (Purists would say, 'Tear the leaves by hand as otherwise the chicory will taste bitter,' but I have never found this to be the case.)

Halve the avocados and remove the stones. Scoop out the

flesh with a teaspoon and sprinkle with a little lemon juice. Combine the vegetables and dressing and mix in the chopped walnuts. Sprinkle a little paprika over the top.

Carinthian cabbage salad

Quite different from the usual salad made with white cabbage, but it has to be prepared just before being served.

1 small firm white cabbage	1 teaspoon caraway seeds
salt	sour cream

Remove any discoloured outer leaves from the cabbage. Quarter the cabbage and discard any 'woody' parts in the centre. Shred the cabbage finely, either with a mandoline cutter or using a food processor. Sprinkle the shredded cabbage with salt and work the salt into the cabbage with your hands. Taste and add more salt if necessary. Mix in the caraway seeds and as much sour cream as the cabbage will absorb. Serve at once.

Mushroom and tomato salad

1 tablespoon olive oil	1 tablespoon chopped chervil
½ lb (225g) mushrooms,	or parsley
sliced	1 shallot, grated
4 dessertspoons olive oil	4 large tomatoes, skinned and
1 dessertspoon wine vinegar	sliced
salt and pepper	2 hardboiled eggs
1 teaspoon French mustard	

Heat the tablespoon of olive oil and simmer the sliced mushrooms gently in this until tender – about 10 minutes. Leave to cool. Make a vinaigrette with the olive oil, the wine vinegar, salt, pepper, French mustard and the chopped chervil or parsley. Add the grated shallot. Mix together well, then add the mushrooms and tomatoes and sprinkle with coarsely chopped hardboiled eggs.

Mushroom salad

¾ lb (350g) button
  mushrooms
1 tablespoon lemon juice
1 tablespoon white wine
  vinegar
4 tablespoons sour cream

1 tablespoon yoghourt
1–2 tablespoons olive oil
salt and white pepper
cayenne pepper
2 tablespoons chopped
  chives

Clean the button mushrooms and slice them into a bowl. Whisk together the lemon juice, wine vinegar, sour cream, yoghourt and oil until well blended. Season with salt, white pepper and the merest flick of cayenne. Add 1 tablespoon chopped chives and mix the dressing with the mushrooms. Sprinkle the remaining chopped chives over the top.

Mushroom and chicken salad

1 carrot
1 onion
sprig each of thyme and
  marjoram
a few lovage leaves
salt and pepper
2 boned chicken breast
  fillets
2 tablespoons olive oil
1 medium-sized onion, finely
  chopped
3–4 oz (80–100g) button
  mushrooms
3 tablespoons olive oil

1 tablespoon white wine
  vinegar
3–4 anchovy fillets
1 heaped teaspoon green
  peppercorns
1 teaspoon Dijon mustard
1 heaped tablespoon
  chopped parsley
to garnish: peeled, sliced
  avocado pear moistened
  with lemon juice and slices
  of hardboiled egg

Put the carrot, onion, thyme, marjoram and lovage leaves into a saucepan, cover with water and simmer gently until the vegetables are soft. Add the salt and pepper and gently poach the chicken fillets in the liquid until they are just cooked (the liquid will make excellent stock).

Meanwhile heat the olive oil and soften the chopped onion in this. Do not allow it to brown. As soon as the chicken fillets are cooked, lift them out of the stock and cut them into strips. Slice the button mushrooms. Pour the oil with the softened onion into a bowl, add the 3 tablespoons oil, the wine vinegar and the anchovy fillets. Put the green peppercorns into a small sieve and rinse them under a cold tap to get rid of excess salt, then add them to the anchovy fillets. Mash the anchovy fillets and the green peppercorns with a fork, beat in the mustard and some pepper – salt should not be necessary since it is provided by the anchovies, but taste to make sure. Beat everything well together, then toss the chicken strips and the mushrooms in the dressing and sprinkle with the chopped parsley. Chill well and serve garnished with slices of avocado pear sprinkled with a little lemon juice to preserve the colour, and slices of hardboiled egg.

Spiced chicken salad

2 oranges
½ lb (225g) cooked chicken
   meat (without skin or
   bone)

6 oz (160g) mayonnaise
a handful blanched almonds
good dash of brandy
salt and white pepper

Rinse the oranges and dry them well, then grate some of the rind until you have about two heaped teaspoons. Peel the oranges and divide into segments, then remove all the skin and pith. Cut the oranges into slices. Cut the chicken meat into thin strips. Mix the grated orange rind with the mayonnaise, add a good dash of brandy. Fold the orange pieces, almonds and sliced chicken into the mayonnaise, taste and adjust seasoning if necessary by adding salt and pepper. Sometimes I add the merest touch of curry, but be careful not to overdo it!

Summer salad

2–3 large tomatoes
4 tablespoons olive oil
1 tablespoon white wine
  vinegar
salt and pepper
1 heaped teaspoon French
  mustard, Dijon for
  preference
1 heaped tablespoon finely
  chopped fresh basil
1 lb (450g) potatoes

a handful cooked French
  beans
1 green or red pepper,
  deseeded and cut into
  strips
10–12 stoned olives
1 tin tuna fish
4–5 hardboiled eggs, cut
  into quarters
strips of anchovy

Choose gnarly shaped tomatoes – their flavour is infinitely better than that of the perfectly shaped round ones which usually taste of nothing at all. Scald the tomatoes with hot water or hold them over a flame for a second or two until the skin 'pops'. Skin the tomatoes and cut them into slices. Make a French dressing by combining the olive oil, vinegar, salt, pepper and French mustard and pour over the tomatoes. Add the chopped basil, mix and then cover the dish and leave it in a cool place while preparing the rest of the salad.

Cook the potatoes in their skins, peel and slice them while they are still hot and add them to the tomatoes. Also add the French beans (merely break them into convenient pieces – do not slice them), the green or red pepper and the olives, cut into halves or quarters. Add the tuna fish – do not flake it, just break it up roughly with a fork. Put the quartered eggs on top and garnish with strips of anchovy.

Apples in wine

Apples cooked in this way were very popular in the eighteenth century as an accompaniment to meat or game.

9 oz (250g) sugar
10 fl oz (280ml) medium-dry
  white wine
juice of 1 lemon
2 cloves
a small stick cinnamon

a few slivers of lemon peel
2 lb (900g) small eating
  apples
cranberry jelly or cranberry
  preserve

Dissolve the sugar in the wine over a low flame. Add the lemon juice, cloves, cinnamon and the lemon peel and simmer gently for about 8 minutes.

Peel, core and halve the apples. Poach the apples gently in the wine until they are transparent. Lift them out carefully and arrange them in a dish, cut side uppermost. Leave the liquid to cool a little, then strain it over the apples. Put a small portion of cranberry jelly or preserve into the centre of each apple. As an accompaniment to meat or game they are best served slightly warm, but they also make an excellent pudding – in which case I prefer them chilled.

Aubergine cream

A rather unusual accompaniment to meat – or fish – but excellent too as a starter in its own right.

2 medium-sized aubergines	½ wineglass
1 heaped tablespoon butter	ul dry sherry
1 tablespoon butter	salt and pepper
a small handful ground	small pinch icing sugar
walnuts	9 fl oz (¼ litre) cream

Peel the aubergines and cut them into cubes. Melt the heaped tablespoon butter in a saucepan, add the cubed aubergines and brown them very lightly in the butter, turning them frequently. At the same time melt the tablespoon of butter in a frying pan and stir in the ground walnuts. Brown the walnuts in the butter, then add them to the aubergines. Add the sherry, cover the pan with a lid and leave to simmer gently until the aubergines are soft. Season with salt, pepper and a small pinch of icing sugar. Leave to get cold. Whisk the cream until stiff and then fold into the cold aubergine mixture.

Egg and horseradish relish

This makes an excellent accompaniment to hot or cold meat.

4 hardboiled eggs	salt
5 fl oz (140ml) sour cream	a little paprika
1 tablespoon freshly grated	
horseradish	

Chop the eggs. Stir in the sour cream and grated horseradish and add salt to taste. Sprinkle a little paprika over the top.

Fresh cucumber sauce

Particularly good with fish, but also excellent with lamb.

1 flat tablespoon mustard
  seeds
4 fl oz (110ml) good stock
1 large cucumber

1 tablespoon butter
dash of wine vinegar
2 tablespoons cream
1 tablespoon chopped dill

Soak the mustard seeds in the stock for 1–2 hours. Halve the cucumber – do not peel it – and remove the seeds. Chop the cucumber finely. Melt the butter in a thick saucepan, add the cucumber and simmer for a minute or so until it becomes transparent. Strain in the stock and cook in an uncovered saucepan until most of the stock has reduced and the cucumber is only just tender. Be careful not to overcook it. Add the wine vinegar and stir, then add the cream and the freshly chopped dill. Allow to blend well and adjust seasoning if necessary. Serve at once.

Mustard sauce

1 finely chopped shallot
1 dessertspoon finely
  chopped parsley
2 lightly heaped tablespoons
  Dijon mustard

2 tablespoons lemon juice
salt and pepper
4 hardboiled egg yolks
4 tablespoons olive oil
pinch powdered saffron

Mix together the chopped shallot, the parsley and the Dijon mustard and push through a fine sieve. Stir in the lemon juice, salt, pepper and the hardboiled egg yolks. Stand the bowl over crushed ice and gradually stir in the olive oil. Add a small pinch of saffron.

Spiced vegetable sauce

Splendid for pasta of all kinds, but also very good as an accompaniment to hot or cold meat.

1 green pepper	3–4 skinned and diced
1 red pepper	tomatoes
2 tablespoons olive oil	salt
1 thinly sliced leek	pinch of sugar
1 large carrot cut into small	a dessertspoon each of
dice	chopped basil, lovage and
1 thick slice of celeriac, diced	marjoram
1 large onion, finely chopped	a pinch of chopped thyme
1 crushed clove garlic	

Deseed and dice the green and red peppers. Heat the olive oil in a thick saucepan, add the leek, carrot, celeriac, onion, peppers and crushed garlic. Simmer gently, stirring constantly, until the vegetables are tender. If necessary, add a little water – just enough to prevent burning. Now add the skinned and diced tomatoes (choose the fat, irregular shaped ones for better flavour), salt and a good pinch of sugar, plus the chopped herbs. Simmer very gently until the tomatoes are just cooked – no more.

Uncooked tomato sauce

5–6 large tomatoes
1 tablespoon finely chopped
  parsley
1 tablespoon finely chopped
  basil

dash of red wine
1–2 tablespoons olive oil
salt and pepper
1 crushed clove garlic

Scald the tomatoes with boiling water, then rinse them in cold water. Remove the skins, slice the tomatoes, put them in a sieve or colander and rinse under cold water to remove the pips. Chop the tomatoes into smallish dice and put into a bowl. Add the parsley and basil, stir in the wine and the olive oil and season with salt and pepper and the crushed clove of garlic. Cover the bowl and chill for at least 4 hours before using.

Caramel punch

9 oz (250g) sugar
18 fl oz (500ml) water
1 orange cut into thin slices
1 bottle red wine (Italian
  Toscanello is excellent for
  this)

8 fl oz (225ml) dark rum
grated rind and juice of 1
  lemon
a little cinnamon bark
1 wineglassful brandy
orange slices for decoration

Melt the sugar in just enough of the water to dissolve it, bring to the boil and throw in the sliced orange. Caramelize the sugar and the orange slices lightly – then remove from the heat and carefully pour in the water, wine and rum. Add lemon rind and juice, cinnamon bark and the brandy. Simmer very gently until the caramel has dissolved, and then strain into a heated punchbowl or a soup terrine and serve at once, with thin slices of orange floating on top.

Hot punch

5–6 tablespoons caster sugar
9 fl oz (250ml) water
2 bottles red wine
finely grated rind of 1 orange
    and ½ lemon

strained juice of 3 oranges
    and 1 lemon
a good dash of Drambuie

Melt the sugar in the water over low heat, then leave to simmer for about a quarter of an hour. Add the wine, together with the lemon juice and rind and orange juice and rind. Cover and leave to stand for several hours, then heat gently, adding a good dash of Drambuie. Strain into a heated punchbowl or a soup terrine and serve at once.

Summer wine

1 orange
1 lemon
1 small grapefruit
6 tablespoons icing sugar
½ wineglassful brandy

½ wineglassful gin
1 tablespoon Grand Marnier
1½ bottles medium-dry red
    wine
soda water

Rinse the fruit quickly under a hot tap, then cut it into thin slices (halve the grapefruit first). Put the slices into a large jug, sprinkle with the icing sugar and add the brandy, gin and Grand Marnier. Pour on the wine, cover the jug and set it to chill for at least 2 hours. To serve, pour as much – or as little – as you like into a glass and top up with chilled soda water.

Puddings

Apple caramel pudding

2 lb (900g) small eating
  apples
4 oz (110g) butter
7 oz (195g) caster sugar
7 fl oz (195ml) cream

1 flat teaspoon vanilla sugar
2 eggs
3 oz (85g) caster sugar
butter for the dish

Lightly butter a deep gratin dish. Peel, core and slice the apples. Melt the 4 oz butter in a pan, add the sliced apples and simmer them gently over a low flame until they have softened slightly – do not let them disintegrate. Add the 7 oz caster sugar, stir very gently and allow the sugar to caramelize. Transfer the apples and the caramel to the lightly buttered gratin dish.

Mix together the cream with a pinch of vanilla sugar, the eggs and the 3 oz of caster sugar. Whisk until well blended, then pour over the apples. Stand the dish in a roasting tin with water to come halfway up the gratin dish. Bake at Gas Mark 4 (350°F) for about 25 minutes. Allow to cool slightly before serving.

Apples in cream
(an eighteenth-century recipe)

6 small eating apples
1 tablespoon flour
2 tablespoons butter
2–3 tablespoons caster or
  icing sugar
1 teaspoon powdered
  cinnamon

1 teaspoon grated lemon rind
2 tablespoons currants or
  raisins
4 egg yolks
9 fl oz (250ml) cream
butter for the dish

Peel, core and slice the apples thinly. Dust the apples with flour and fry in the butter until golden brown. Butter a deep gratin dish. Arrange the apples in the dish, sprinkle with sugar and cinnamon and then sprinkle the grated lemon rind and the currants or raisins over the apples.

Whisk together the egg yolks and cream and pour over the apples. Stand the dish in a large baking tin with water to come halfway up the gratin dish. Bake at Gas Mark 4 (350°F) until golden brown. Allow to cool slightly before serving.

Apple gratin

1 lb (450g) small eating
  apples
½ pint (275ml) white wine
½ pint (275ml) water
1 tablespoon icing sugar
grated lemon rind
2 eggs
2 heaped tablespoons icing
  sugar

pinch vanilla sugar
7 fl oz (200ml) cream
3 tablespoons biscuit crumbs
3 tablespoons ground
  walnuts or hazelnuts
icing sugar
butter for the dish

Peel, core and halve the apples and then poach them in a mixture of water and white wine to which a tablespoon of icing sugar and a little grated lemon rind has been added. Drain the apples – save the juice, it is excellent for fruit salads – and arrange the apples in a buttered gratin dish, cut side downwards.

Preheat the oven to Gas Mark 5 (375°F). Separate the yolks and whites of the eggs. Whisk the egg yolks with the icing sugar until very thick and creamy. Add the vanilla sugar, then whisk in the cream. Fold in the biscuit crumbs (crushed boudoir biscuits are particularly good for this recipe). Whisk the egg whites until stiff and fold into the mixture, alternately with the ground walnuts or hazelnuts. Pile the mixture on top of the apples and bake until nicely browned on top. Dust with icing sugar or – for special occasions – serve with ice-cold, lightly sweetened whipped cream.

Bolzano apples
(6 portions)

2 tablespoons sugar
9 fl oz (250ml) dry white
  wine
vanilla pod
6 small eating apples
6 egg yolks

½ teaspoon vanilla sugar
5½ oz (150g) icing sugar
1 tablespoon rum
8 fl oz (225ml) cream
a few crushed macaroons or
  Amaretti biscuits

Dissolve the 2 tablespoons of sugar in the wine, add the vanilla pod and heat gently. Peel, core and halve the apples. Poach the apples gently in the liquid (do not allow them to overcook). Lift out the apple halves and arrange them in a bowl – or in

138

separate small bowls. Whisk together the egg yolks, vanilla sugar and icing sugar until thick and fluffy, then gradually add the liquid from the apples and a good dash of rum. Whisk in the cream and spoon over the apples. Chill for at least 1 hour before serving. At the last moment sprinkle a few crushed macaroons or Amaretti biscuits over the top.

Apricot pudding

1 lb (450g) apricots
4½ fl oz (125ml) white wine
2 tablespoons sugar
4 eggs
3 oz (80g) icing sugar
2 oz (60g) ground walnuts or hazelnuts

1 scant oz (25g) fine breadcrumbs
1½ oz (40g) melted butter
butter and breadcrumbs for the dish

Butter a large gratin dish and dust it with fine breadcrumbs or ground hazelnuts.

Stone the apricots and poach them in the wine with 2 tablespoons sugar until they are just tender – do not overcook them. (Two or three crushed apricot stones – the brown skin comes off quite easily – poached with the apricots greatly improve the flavour.)

Separate the egg yolks and whites. Whisk the whites until stiff, then whisk in half the icing sugar until well blended. Whisk in the egg yolks one by one and then whisk in the remaining sugar. Fold in the ground walnuts or hazelnuts and the breadcrumbs. Finally fold in the melted, but not hot butter.

Put half the mixture into the buttered gratin dish, cover with the apricots and pile the remaining mixture on top. Bake at

Gas Mark 5 (375°F) and for the first 10 minutes of the baking time leave the oven door the smallest bit open – just do not close it properly. After that time close the oven door and bake the pudding until it is golden brown on top. It tastes equally good hot or cold, but I prefer it when it is just warm, with a fine sprinkling of vanilla sugar on top.

Baked peaches

5 large peaches	2 tablespoons chocolate
2 oz (60g) macaroons or	powder
Amaretti biscuits	butter for the dish
a good dash of rum	small flakes of butter
2 tablespoons icing or	icing sugar
caster sugar	½ cup brandy
1 small egg	

Wipe over the peaches – do not remove the skins. Halve the peaches, remove the stones and scrape out a little of the peach flesh with a teaspoon. Crush the macaroons (or Amaretti biscuits) and moisten with rum. Crush the scooped out peach flesh with a fork and mix with the soaked crumbs. Add the sugar, beat in the egg and the chocolate powder.

Butter a deep gratin dish and set the peach halves side by side in the dish. Fill the centre with the biscuit mixture and dot with small flakes of butter. Bake at Gas Mark 5 (375°F) for 20–30 minutes. Dust with icing sugar. Gently heat the brandy, pour over the peaches and set alight.

Cherry cream

1 lb (450g) black or Morello
   cherries
3–4 oz (85–110g) icing
   or caster sugar
16 fl oz (450ml) milk
3 tablespoons sugar
a pinch of vanilla sugar

4 egg yolks
2 fl oz (60ml) milk
1 heaped teaspoon cornflour
2 egg whites
5 fl oz (140ml) cream
5–6 crushed Amaretti biscuits
   or 2 crushed meringues

Stone the cherries and sprinkle with the icing or caster sugar. Morello cherries will need a little more sugar than black cherries. Leave them to stand in a cool place for about 1 hour. Gently simmer the cherries in their own juice for about 5 minutes. Put the cooked cherries into a bowl or into individual bowls and chill.

Gently heat the 16 fl oz milk with the 3 tablespoons of sugar and the vanilla sugar. Whisk together the egg yolks, the 2 fl oz milk and cornflour. Pour on the warmed milk, whisking all the time. Return the mixture to the stove and cook it very gently until thick (you can use a double saucepan for this, but it is not strictly necessary, provided a little care is taken). Remove from the stove then allow to cool, stirring from time to time. When the mixture is quite cold, whisk the egg whites until stiff. Also whisk the cream. Fold the egg whites and cream into the egg custard, together with the crushed Amaretti biscuits or the meringues. Spoon the cream over the cherries and chill before serving.

Black cherry pudding

4–5 rolls, at least one day old
9 fl oz (250ml) lukewarm
  milk
1½ lb (700g) black cherries
4 oz (110g) butter
4 oz (110g) sugar
3 eggs
1 teaspoon cinnamon
1 scant teaspoon grated
  lemon rind
2½ oz (70g) ground almonds
vanilla sugar
butter for the dish

Preheat the oven to Gas Mark 5 (375°F). Grate the crust off the rolls and then slice the rolls fairly thinly. Pour the milk over the rolls and leave to stand. Wash and dry the cherries, remove the stalks but do not stone them.

Cream 3½ oz of the butter with the sugar. Separate the egg yolks and whites and beat the egg yolks into the creamed butter, one by one. Add cinnamon and lemon rind. Beat in the softened rolls. Whisk the egg whites until stiff, fold into the mixture alternately with half the ground almonds. Fold in the cherries.

Put the mixture into a buttered gratin dish and sprinkle with the remaining almonds. Dot with small flakes of the remaining butter. Bake for 45–55 minutes until well browned. Dust with vanilla sugar and allow to cool a little before serving.

Pudding made with fresh plums

1½ lb (675g) plums
3 tablespoons caster or icing
  sugar
1 teaspoon vanilla sugar
pinch of cinnamon and
  allspice

1 oz (25g) ground almonds
1 tablespoon cream
dash of rum
butter for the dish

FOR THE TOPPING
3 eggs
2 oz (60g) butter
2½ oz (70g) caster or icing
  sugar

5 fl oz (140ml) milk
3½ oz (100g) flour
1 teaspoon vanilla sugar
grated lemon rind

Lightly butter a soufflé or deep gratin dish. Stone and halve the plums and put them into the dish, sprinkle with sugar, vanilla sugar, spice and ground almonds. Add the cream and the rum and stir lightly, then cover the dish and leave to stand for at least half an hour – longer if possible.

Preheat the oven to Gas Mark 2 (300°F) and put the dish with the plums, still covered, into the oven while preparing the topping.

Separate the egg yolks and whites. Cream the butter and sugar until light and fluffy, then beat in the egg yolks one by one. Gradually beat in the milk and the flour. Whisk the egg whites until stiff, then fold the egg whites into the butter and egg mixture, together with the vanilla sugar and the grated lemon rind. Pile the mixture on top of the plums which should have heated through by now. Bake for 15 minutes at Gas Mark 2 (300°F), then increase the heat to Gas Mark 4 (350°F) and eventually to Gas Mark 5 (375°F). Total baking time: ¾–1 hour. The juice at the bottom of the dish, which may at first look as if

THE SUNDAY EXPRESS COOKBOOK

the pudding had not quite baked through, is in fact the plums having formed their own delicious sauce, together with the cream and the almonds. The pudding tastes equally good served hot, cold or just warm.

Plum and almond pudding

1 lb (450g) plums, Victoria for preference
2–3 tablespoons soft brown sugar
pinch each of powdered cinnamon and cloves
3 oz (85g) boudoir biscuits (about 16–18 biscuits)
3½ oz (100g) ground unblanched almonds
3 eggs
2½ oz (70g) icing or caster sugar
1 teaspoon vanilla sugar
1 tablespoon rum

Halve the plums and remove the stones. Put the plums into a fairly deep gratin dish and sprinkle them with the brown sugar, cinnamon and cloves. Cover and leave to stand for as long as possible – the longer the better. Put the dish – still covered – into the oven at Gas Mark 3 (325°F) until they are just cooked but still retain their shape.

Crush the boudoir biscuits with a rolling pin (or use a coffee mill or food grinder) until they are the consistency of rather coarse breadcrumbs. Mix together the crushed biscuits and the ground almonds. Separate the egg yolks and whites. Whisk together the egg yolks, sugar and vanilla sugar until thick and creamy. Add the rum. Whisk the egg whites until stiff. Fold the whipped egg whites into the egg yolks, alternately with the biscuit crumbs and ground almond mixture. Pile on top of the plums and bake at Gas Mark 4 (350°F) until nicely browned on top – about 30 minutes. Serve hot with thick ice-cold cream – though it is pretty good cold, too, even without the cream.

144

Glacé fruit pudding

8 oz (225g) boudoir biscuits
¼ pint (140ml) cream
1 vanilla pod
3½ oz (100g) butter
3½ oz (100g) caster sugar
3 eggs

5 oz (140g) mixed glacé fruit,
   cut into small pieces
4 tablespoons apricot jam
butter and biscuit crumbs for
   the pudding basin
1 tablespoon Cointreau

Crumble the boudoir biscuits into a bowl. Heat the cream with the vanilla pod until almost boiling and pour over the boudoir biscuits. Leave to cool and then remove the vanilla pod.

Cream the butter and sugar until light and fluffy. Separate the egg yolks and whites. Beat the yolks into the creamed butter, one by one. Gradually beat in the soaked boudoir biscuits and the glacé fruit. Whisk the egg whites until stiff and fold into the mixture. Pour the mixture into a buttered and crumbed pudding basin. Cover with foil, leaving room for expansion and steam for 1 hour.

Heat the jam until melted and then sieve it. Stir in the Cointreau. Turn the pudding on to a heated platter and serve with the apricot sauce.

Chestnut pudding

10 oz (280g) peeled, cooked
   chestnuts
5 oz (140g) butter
4 oz (110g) icing or caster
   sugar
6 eggs

4 oz (110g) ground almonds
pinch cinnamon
finely grated rind of 1 lemon
icing sugar for dusting over
   the pudding
butter and sugar for the dish

Chestnuts canned in water can be used for this (drain them well before use). If you start 'from scratch', using chestnuts in their skins, you will need about 1 lb (450g) unskinned chestnuts to achieve the 10 oz peeled ones required for the recipe. Tinned chestnut purée – even if it is unsweetened – is not suitable for this recipe as it is too soft.

Preheat the oven to Gas Mark 5 (375°F). Butter a deep gratin dish and dust it lightly with sugar. Sieve the butter with the sugar until light and fluffy. Separate the egg yolks and whites. Beat the egg yolks into the sugar and butter mixture, one by one, beating well after each addition, adding a little of the ground almonds if the mixture shows any sign of curdling. Beat in the chestnut purée, cinnamon and lemon rind. Whisk the egg whites until stiff and fold into the mixture, alternately with the remaining ground almonds. Pile the mixture into the gratin dish and bake for about 30 minutes – until nicely browned on top. Serve warm rather than hot, sprinkled thickly with icing sugar. A frothy wine sauce such as the one suggested with the brown bread pudding (see page 157) goes well with this, as does a simple chocolate sauce.

Baked walnut pudding

butter and ground walnuts
for the dish
3½ oz (100g) cottage cheese
6 eggs
3½ oz (100g) butter
3½ oz (100g) caster or icing
sugar

3½ oz (100g) ground walnuts
3½ oz (100g) raisins
a little grated lemon rind
1 teaspoon vanilla sugar
icing sugar for the top

Butter a deep dish and dust it lightly with ground walnuts. Preheat the oven to Gas Mark 5 (375°F).

Sieve the cottage cheese so that it is absolutely free from lumps and very smooth. Separate the egg yolks and whites. Cream the butter and sugar until light and fluffy, then beat in the cottage cheese and the egg yolks, adding them one by one and beating well after each addition. Whisk the egg whites until stiff and fold into the mixture, alternately with the ground walnuts. Finally fold in the raisins, grated lemon rind and vanilla sugar. Arrange the mixture in the gratin dish and bake until nicely browned on top. Dust thickly with icing sugar and leave to cool a little before serving – it tastes best when eaten just warm, not hot.

Soufflé for two

3 oz (85g) crystallized fruit	1 heaped tablespoon butter
a good dash of Kirsch	1 heaped tablespoon flour
¼ pint (140ml) milk	2 egg yolks
1 teaspoon vanilla sugar	3 egg whites
2 tablespoons caster or icing sugar	butter and icing or caster sugar for the dish

Preheat the oven to Gas Mark 7 (425°F). Butter a soufflé dish and dust it lightly with caster or icing sugar. Cut the crystallized fruit into small chunks and moisten it with a good dash of Kirsch.

Put the milk into a small saucepan, add the vanilla sugar, 1 tablespoon of the caster or icing sugar and the butter. Stir to dissolve the sugar, then heat slowly so that the butter has melted completely when the milk comes to the boil. Tip in the flour and stir the mixture over a low flame until it is smooth and begins to leave the sides of the saucepan clean. Remove from the heat and gradually beat in the egg yolks. Whisk the egg whites until stiff, then whisk in the remaining sugar. Fold the whites into the yolk mixture and then fold in the crystallized fruit. Pile the mixture into the prepared soufflé dish and bake until well risen and golden brown – about 10–12 minutes. Serve at once, preferably with a good vanilla cream.

'The gentle pudding'

The quantities given should be enough for three or even four, but this pudding is so light and delicious that I have known two people polish it off without any difficulty whatsoever – almost absentmindedly as it were – so be warned!

3 eggs	3 tablespoons cream
2 tablespoons icing or caster sugar	1 tablespoon flour
1 teaspoon vanilla sugar	a little grated orange rind
	butter and flour for the dish

Butter and lightly flour a deep gratin or soufflé dish. Preheat the oven to Gas Mark 5 (375°F). Separate the egg yolks and whites. Whisk together the yolks, sugar and vanilla sugar until thick and creamy, then whisk in the cream. Whisk the whites until very stiff, then fold them into the yolks, alternately with the flour. Finally sprinkle in the grated orange rind. Pile the mixture into the prepared dish and bake until nicely browned on top – about 12–15 minutes. Serve at once, spooning out from the sides. The mixture should still be a little runny inside and it will go on cooking a bit in the hot dish, so that second helpings will be just right when you get round to them.

The simple pudding

⅜ pint (200ml) coarse
  semolina
3 eggs
2 heaped tablespoons caster
  sugar
1 teaspoon vanilla sugar
1 heaped tablespoon butter
27 fl oz (750ml) cold milk

3 tablespoons caster sugar
pinch vanilla sugar
2 teaspoons grated orange
  rind
butter for the dishes
sugar for sprinkling over the
  top

The most important 'ingredients' for this delectable pudding
are two gratin dishes, one of which should be slightly larger
and deeper than the other. Butter both dishes fairly well.
Preheat the oven to Gas Mark 4 (350°F). Measure out the
semolina – it is quicker and easier to use a measuring jug than
to weigh it.

Whisk together the eggs with the 2 tablespoons of sugar and
the vanilla sugar until light and frothy, then fold in the
semolina – just pour it in gently from the measuring jug. Bake
the mixture in the smaller of the two dishes until golden
brown on top and just a little firm to the touch – about 15
minutes.

Put the heaped tablespoon of butter in a cup and stand this
in a pan of hot water so that the butter melts.

As soon as the semolina mixture is golden brown, tip it
carefully into the larger dish while it is still hot. Mix together
the cold milk, sugar and vanilla sugar, grated orange rind and
stir in the melted butter. Pour this over the baked pudding – it
should cover it completely. Lower the oven heat to Gas Mark 3
(325°F) and put the dish in the oven until the milk has been
completely absorbed. Serve sprinkled thickly with sugar. It is
intended to be eaten hot, but it is also delicious cold,
particularly if served with a good fruit syrup.

'Tommerl'

A wonderfully warming pudding from Styria, the basis being coarsely ground maize, sometimes sold under the name of Polenta. Some shops sell two kinds, finely and coarsely ground. Choose the coarsely ground maize for this pudding.

Quantities are for 4–6 generous helpings, but I find that any leftover pudding seems to disappear with lightning speed, just eaten cold!

1 pint (575ml) milk
5 heaped tablespoons caster
   sugar
vanilla pod
¼ pint (140ml) coarsely
   ground maize
3 heaped tablespoons butter

3 eggs
juice of ½ lemon
a little grated lemon rind
pinch of cinnamon
butter and flour for the
   baking dish

I have given the measurement for the maize in liquid rather than in solid measures since pouring the maize into the hot milk is easier when done straight from a measuring jug.

Heat the milk with 1 tablespoon of the sugar and the vanilla pod. Just as the milk is rising to the top, pour in the ground maize and cook it, stirring all the time, until the mixture is very thick. Pour into a bowl and leave to cool. Remove the vanilla pod.

Cream together the butter and 3 tablespoons of the sugar. Separate the eggs. Beat the yolks gradually into the creamed butter, then add the lemon juice, grated lemon rind and cinnamon. Beat in the cooled maize mixture. Whisk the egg whites until stiff and then whisk in the remaining sugar. Fold the whipped egg whites into the maize mixture, pour into a buttered and lightly floured gratin dish and bake at Gas Mark 4

(350°F) for about 1 hour. It is delicious just as it is or served with fruit syrup or purée, but you can also add some fruit to the mixture before it is baked – thinly sliced apples or a small tin of drained cherries, for instance, or simply some raisins or sultanas – particularly good if previously soaked in a little rum.

Vanilla pudding
(serve 3–4)

3 eggs
1 tablespoon flour
⅜ pint (210ml) milk
1½ oz (40g) butter

2 oz (50g) icing sugar
1 teaspoon vanilla sugar
butter and flour for the dish

Preheat the oven to Gas Mark 7 (425°F). Butter and flour a soufflé dish. Separate the egg yolks and whites. Blend together the flour and yolks, then add a little of the milk. Heat the remaining milk with the butter and the sugars and stir into the egg yolks. Return the mixture to the stove in a double boiler, or – if you are very careful – cook it very gently over direct heat until thickened (if you are not very careful it will curdle!). Remove from the heat, leave to cool, stirring occasionally. Whisk the egg whites until stiff and fold into the mixture. Bake for about 12 minutes. Serve at once.

Vienna pudding

5 oz (140g) butter
4 oz (120g) caster or icing
  sugar
1 teaspoon vanilla sugar
7 egg yolks

4 oz (120g) ground
  almonds
4 egg whites
butter and sugar (or ground
  almonds) for the dish

FOR THE SAUCE
¼ pint (140ml) white wine
2½ oz (70g) caster sugar

dash of lemon juice
2 eggs

Butter a pudding bowl and lightly dust with sugar or ground almonds.

Cream the butter, sugar and vanilla sugar until light and fluffy, then beat in the egg yolks one by one, beating well after each addition. Gradually add half the ground almonds. Whisk the egg whites until stiff and fold into the mixture, alternately with the remaining ground almonds. Steam for about ¾ hour – until well risen and slightly firm to the touch. Carefully turn out on to a warmed serving dish and serve with the following sauce: whisk together over steam – in a large bowl since the mixture will expand considerably – the wine, sugar, lemon juice and eggs until very light and frothy. Serve at once.

Wine pudding

3 eggs
3 lightly heaped tablespoons
  icing sugar
3–4 lightly heaped
  tablespoons ground
  walnuts
a little rum
½ pint (275ml) medium-dry
  red wine
¼ pint (140ml) water

3 tablespoons sugar
a vanilla pod or 1 teaspoon
  vanilla sugar
2 cloves
a little cinnamon rind
2 teaspoons grated orange
  rind
butter and flour for the cake
  tin

Butter and flour an 8 or 9 inch cake tin. Preheat the oven to Gas Mark 4 (350°F).

Separate the egg yolks and whites. Whisk the yolks with the icing sugar until thick and fluffy. Whisk the whites until stiff. Fold the whipped whites into the yolks, alternately with the ground walnuts, moistened with a little rum. (You can use fine breadcrumbs instead of the walnuts – or a mixture of both, but be extra-generous with the rum in that case.) Tip the mixture into the prepared cake tin and bake for about 45 minutes – until the top feels slightly firm and the 'cake' has shrunk away slightly from the sides of the tin.

While the mixture is baking put the wine and the water into a saucepan, add the sugar, vanilla pod (or vanilla sugar), the cloves, cinnamon rind and grated orange rind. Heat gently until the sugar has dissolved, and leave to simmer until the cake is baked.

Carefully remove the cake from the tin and set it on a warmed, deep serving dish. Slowly strain the hot wine over it. Serve warm.

153

Rum pudding

a good tablespoon rum
2½ oz (70g) butter
2½ oz (70g) icing sugar
3 eggs
2½ oz (70g) ground
 unblanched almonds
2½ oz (70g) raisins

1 oz (28g) grated chocolate
1 scant oz (25g) fine
 breadcrumbs
butter and ground
 unblanched almonds for
 the pudding basin

FOR THE SAUCE
2 egg yolks
3 tablespoons rum

2 tablespoons caster sugar
½ teaspoon vanilla sugar

Butter a pudding basin and dust lightly with ground unblanched almonds. Pour the rum over the breadcrumbs and
leave to soak.

Cream the butter with the sugar until light and fluffy.
Separate the egg yolks and whites. Beat the yolks – one by one
– into the butter and sugar mixture. Beat in the chocolate and
the breadcrumbs moistened with rum. Whisk the egg whites
until stiff and fold into the mixture, alternately with the ground
almonds and the raisins. Pile the mixture into the prepared
pudding basin and steam gently for about ¾ hour. Set the
pudding on a warmed dish and serve with rum sauce prepared
as follows: whisk together over steam the egg yolks, rum, sugar
and vanilla sugar until thick and fluffy.

Bohemian bun pudding

Served with ice-cold vanilla cream this makes a delectable pudding for a cold day.

FOR THE BUNS
scant ½ pint (250ml) milk
¾ oz (20g) fresh yeast
¾ oz (20g) caster sugar
1 lb (500g) plain strong flour
2 teaspoons vanilla sugar
1 egg

2 egg yolks
1 tablespoon rum
1 teaspoon grated orange
 rind
1 oz (30g) ground almonds
5 oz (140g) melted butter

FOR COOKING THE BUNS
1½ oz (45g) butter
1 oz (30g) caster sugar
2 teaspoons vanilla sugar
scant ½ pint (250ml) single
 or double cream

2–3 tablespoons melted
 butter

To make the buns, heat the milk until lukewarm. Cream the yeast with a teaspoon of the sugar, stir in a teaspoon of the flour and about a cupful of the milk. Sift the remaining flour and sugar into a warmed bowl, together with the vanilla sugar. Make a well in the centre and pour in the yeast mixture. Set aside in a warm place for about 10 minutes – until the liquid begins to bubble. Add the remaining milk, draw in the flour and beat in the egg, egg yolks, rum, orange rind, ground almonds and finally the melted butter. Beat well – or use the dough hook of the electric mixer – until you have a smooth shiny dough which leaves the sides of the bowl clean. Cover with a cloth and set aside in a warm place for about 40–50 minutes – until doubled in size.

155

Turn out the dough on to a warmed and floured pastry board and knead lightly. Roll out to about ½ inch thickness and cut into rounds measuring about 2 inches in diameter (you will get about 50 rounds).

Put the butter, sugar, vanilla sugar and cream for cooking the buns into a saucepan and stir over low heat to dissolve the sugar and the butter. Pour this mixture into two large, deep baking dishes. The temperature of the cream mixture should be lukewarm – if necessary allow it to cool. Put the rounds of dough side by side in the dishes and brush the tops with some of the melted butter. Cover the dishes lightly with a cloth and set in a warm place for about 30 minutes – until the buns have doubled in size. Brush over them with the remaining butter and bake in a preheated oven at Gas Mark 5 (375°F) for about 40–45 minutes until nicely browned on top. Serve warm with vanilla sauce.

The princes' pudding

3½ oz (100g) boudoir
   biscuits
3½ oz (100g) macaroons or
   Amaretti biscuits
½ pint (225ml) cream

8 egg yolks
6 egg whites
butter and sugar for the
   dish

FOR THE SAUCE
8 fl oz (225ml) red wine
a small piece cinnamon

1–2 cloves
1 teaspoon sugar

Crush the boudoir biscuits and the macaroons (or Amaretti) to the size of fairly coarse breadcrumbs. Heat the cream, add the crushed biscuits and cook very gently, stirring all the time, until the mixture is thick. Remove from the heat and leave to cool, stirring from time to time. Beat in the egg yolks separately. Whisk the egg whites until stiff, then fold into the mixture. Bake in a buttered and sugared deep baking dish at Gas Mark 3 (325°F) for about 1–1¼ hours.

Heat the wine with the cinnamon, cloves and sugar.

Carefully turn out the pudding on to a heated platter. Either strain the hot wine over it or serve separately.

Brown bread pudding

Cut any leftover brown bread into slices – rye bread is particularly good for this recipe – and let it dry out completely. You may help this along by putting the slices into a barely warm oven, or even into the oven after it has been switched off. Crush the dried bread into crumbs – an electric coffee grinder is excellent for this purpose. The crumbs should be fairly fine so if necessary sift them before use.

4½ fl oz (125ml) red wine
5½ oz (150g) brown
   breadcrumbs
5½ oz (150g) butter
5½ oz (150g) icing sugar
4 eggs
1 teaspoon vanilla sugar
2 teaspoons grated orange
   rind

½ teaspoon powdered
   cinnamon
2 oz (55g) ground walnuts or
   hazelnuts
butter and flour or ground
   walnuts for the pudding
   basin

Butter and lightly flour a pudding basin (or dust with ground walnuts). Pour the wine over the breadcrumbs and leave to stand for about 20 minutes. Cream the butter and icing sugar until light and fluffy. Separate the egg yolks and whites. Beat the yolks into the creamed butter, one by one, beating well after each addition. Also beat in the vanilla sugar, grated orange rind and the cinnamon. Add the soaked breadcrumbs. Whisk the egg whites until stiff and fold into the mixture, alternately with the ground walnuts or hazelnuts. Pile the mixture into the pudding basin, cover with pleated foil so that there is plenty of room for expansion. Steam the pudding very gently for about 1–1½ hours. Turn on to a heated platter and serve with stewed fruit or a good egg custard or – for special occasions – with a red wine sauce made by whisking together over steam 9 fl oz (250ml) red wine, 4 oz (110g) caster sugar, 2 egg yolks and 1 egg. Whisk until very light and frothy and serve at once.

Downy pancakes

My favourite pancakes are featherlight, soft and almost creamy inside. Fruit purée to which a little cream or whipped cream has been added makes an excellent filling, but my own preference is for a thick vanilla custard made with cream.

FOR 4 PANCAKES

4 eggs	pinch salt
1½ oz (40g) butter	1 flat tablespoon icing sugar
1½ oz (40g) flour	butter for frying
13 fl oz (375ml) milk	

Separate the egg yolks and whites. Melt the butter in a saucepan, stir in the flour. The flour should not really brown, just acquire the merest blush of colour. Gradually stir in the milk and a pinch of salt. Bring to the boil, stirring constantly. Remove from the fire, leave to cool a little, then stir in the egg yolks, one by one. Whisk the egg whites until stiff, then whisk in the icing sugar. Fold the egg whites into the egg yolk mixture. Melt a small knob of butter in an omelette pan and pour or ladle in a quarter of the batter. Fry the pancake gently until golden brown on one side, then turn over carefully – no tossing, please – and leave to brown on the other side. Fill as desired, fold over and serve, dusted liberally with icing sugar. Use up the remaining batter in the same way.

Pancake pudding

FOR THE PANCAKES
2 oz (60g) butter
5 eggs
2 oz (60g) icing or caster
  sugar

1 tea cup milk
2 oz (60g) self-raising flour,
  sifted

FOR THE FILLING
3 eggs
3 tablespoons icing sugar
a little grated lemon rind

½ teaspoon vanilla sugar
4 oz (115g) ground almonds

butter and breadcrumbs for
  the cake tin
butter for frying

about 3 fl oz (85ml) sour
  cream for topping
icing sugar for the top

Butter a 9-inch spring-clip cake tin and dust it lightly with fine breadcrumbs.

    Put the butter into a tea cup and stand this in a small pan

with hot water until the butter melts. Separate the egg yolks and whites. Whisk the egg yolks with the sugar until very thick and creamy. Whisk in the milk. Whip the egg whites until stiff and fold into the batter, alternately with the sifted flour. Finally fold in the melted but not hot butter.

To make the filling, separate the egg yolks and whites. Whisk the yolks with the sugar until thick and creamy, add the grated lemon rind and vanilla sugar. Whisk the whites until stiff and fold into the egg yolks alternately with the ground almonds.

Melt a small knob of butter in a frying pan – if possible this should be the same size as the cake tin, though it does not matter if it is slightly smaller in diameter. Pour in a quarter of the batter and fry the pancake until it is golden brown underneath. Slip the pancake – upside down so that the uncooked side rests on the bottom of the cake tin – into the cake tin. This is quite easy with the first pancake as you can simply invert the cake tin over the frying pan, but gets a little more difficult with the subsequent pancakes, though it is in fact easier than it sounds. If necessary, push them gently into place. Spread the cooked side of each pancake with filling before placing the next pancake on top. The top layer should be a pancake – no filling. Spread the top thickly with sour cream and bake the pudding at Gas Mark 6 (400°F) until the cream is just tinged with colour – about 20–25 minutes. Take the cake out of the oven and release the spring clip and dust the top thickly with icing sugar. Do not attempt to remove the pudding from the bottom of the cake tin, just set it on a large serving dish with the cake base still underneath. Serve cut into wedges like a cake.

Pancake pudding made with cottage cheese

1 oz (30g) raisins
a little rum
1½ oz (40g) butter
1½ oz (40g) caster sugar
2 eggs
4½ fl oz (120g) sour cream
7 oz (200g) sieved cottage
  cheese

grated lemon rind
1 teaspoon vanilla sugar
pinch powdered cinnamon
8 thin pancakes, about 8
  inches in diameter
butter for the dish

FOR THE TOPPING
5 fl oz (140ml) sour cream
2 tablespoons milk
1 egg

1 oz (30g) icing or caster
  sugar
icing sugar for the top

Soak the raisins in a little rum to make them swell up. Cream the butter with the caster sugar until fluffy. Separate the egg yolks and whites. Beat the egg yolks into the butter mixture, then beat in the sour cream and the cottage cheese. Also add the lemon rind, vanilla sugar and cinnamon. Whisk the egg whites until stiff and fold into the mixture, then fold in the raisins. Butter a deep gratin dish.

Cut the pancakes in half and spread them thickly with the mixture. Roll up the pancakes very carefully and arrange them – crosswise – in the dish.

Whisk together the sour cream, milk, egg and sugar and pour over the pancakes. Bake at Gas Mark 4 (325°F) for about 25–30 minutes, until the creamy mixture has set. Serve warm – not hot – sprinkled with icing sugar.

Pastries, gâteaux and tarts

Almond pastries

6 oz (170g) flour
5 oz (140g) icing sugar
5 oz (140g) ground
    unblanched almonds
pinch powdered cinnamon
pinch powdered allspice
1 teaspoon grated lemon rind
5 oz (140g) butter

4 hardboiled egg yolks
a little egg white
a little egg yolk
blanched nibbed or slivered
    almonds
cranberry jam
butter and flour for the
    baking sheet

Butter and flour a baking sheet. Preheat the oven to Gas Mark 5 (375°F).

Sift together the flour and sugar. Add the ground almonds, cinnamon, allspice and lemon rind. Rub in the butter and the hardboiled egg yolks (you can use the whites – chopped finely – for sprinkling over a crisp lettuce salad). Roll out the pastry to about ¼ inch thickness and stamp into rounds of 2 inches in diameter. Gather up the offcuts and roll them between the palms of your hands to pencil slimness, then use them to form a small band round each pastry, sealing them down with a little egg white. Brush the pastry with egg yolk and sprinkle with nibbed or slivered almonds. Bake until golden brown. Set to cool on a rack and then fill with cranberry jam.

Gâteau Lorraine

In Lorraine this delectable cake is made with Mirabelles – small, golden plums which are sometimes sold as 'cherry plums' in this country – but it works equally well with greengages.

3 tablespoons sugar
½ pint (265ml) water
1 lb (450g) Mirabelles or
  greengages
4 eggs
7 oz (200g) flour
2 teaspoons baking powder
5 oz (140g) icing or caster
  sugar

1 teaspoon vanilla sugar
16 fl oz (450ml) yoghourt
3 tablespoons Eau de
  Mirabelle (or plum
  brandy)
butter and flour for the
  cake tin

Dissolve the 3 tablespoons of sugar in the water, bring to the boil and then throw in the Mirabelles or greengages. Reduce the heat and poach the plums very gently in the syrup until just cooked. Be careful not to overcook them. Drain the plums. Do not throw away the syrup, though – it will do splendidly for all sorts of summer drinks and fruit salads.

Butter and flour a 10-inch cake tin. Preheat the oven to Gas Mark 4 (350°F).

Separate the egg yolks and whites. Sift the flour with the baking powder. Whisk the yolks with the sugar and vanilla sugar until thick and creamy. Gradually beat in the yoghourt and the Eau de Mirabelle. Whisk the egg whites until stiff and fold in alternately with the flour.

Pour half the mixture into the prepared cake tin, cover with the drained plums and then top with the remaining cake mixture and smooth over the top.

Bake the cake for about 40–45 minutes. Let it cool for a few minutes in the cake tin, then take it out carefully and allow it to cool completely on a rack. It is a lovely moist cake, not too sweet, which can also be served as a pudding – in which case serve a good vanilla custard with it.

Strawberry gâteau

FOR THE CAKE

5 eggs
4½ oz (125g) icing or caster
  sugar
1 teaspoon vanilla sugar

4½ oz (125g) sifted flour
1 teaspoon grated lemon rind
butter and flour for the cake
  tin

FOR THE FILLING

⅓ oz (10g) gelatine crystals
3–4 tablespoons icing sugar
½ lb (225g) strawberry purée
  (sieved strawberries)
1 dessertspoon lemon juice

1 pint (550ml) cream
about 4 tablespoons
  Cointreau
strawberries for decoration
a little icing sugar

Butter and flour a 9- or 10-inch spring-clip cake tin. Preheat the oven to Gas Mark 5 (375°F).

Whisk together over steam the eggs and the icing or caster sugar with the vanilla sugar until very thick and creamy. Remove the bowl from the heat, whisk until cooled, then fold in the sifted flour and the lemon rind. Bake until golden brown and the cake has shrunk away slightly from the sides – about 45–50 minutes.

Carefully remove from the cake tin and set to cool on a rack. When the cake is quite cold – preferably the next day – cut it into three layers. (You can also bake the cake in three separate layers – in which case the heat should be increased to Mark 6/400°F. Baking time will be reduced to about half.)

Dissolve the gelatine in 1 fl oz of hot water. Stir the icing sugar into the strawberry purée until well blended and the sugar has dissolved. Add the lemon juice and dissolved gelatine. Whisk the cream to a soft peak. Set aside enough of the cream for spreading over the cake and fold the remainder into the strawberry purée. Put the first layer of the cake into a spring-clip cake tin and sprinkle it with Cointreau. Spread half the strawberry cream over the base and press a few halved strawberries lightly into it, smoothing the cream mixture over them. Cover with a second layer of cake, sprinkle again with Cointreau and smooth the remaining strawberry cream over it. Cover with the remaining cake layer and set to chill for about an hour. Remove the spring clip and carefully slide the cake on to a serving dish. Whisk a little icing sugar into the remaining whipped cream and spread over the cake. Decorate with whole strawberries.

Hazelnut and strawberry gâteau

FOR THE PASTRY

4 oz (120g) hazelnuts	6 oz (165g) butter
4 oz (120g) caster sugar	butter and flour for the
7 oz (200g) flour	baking sheets

FOR THE FILLING

8 oz (225g) wild strawberries	½ pint (280ml) cream
8 oz (225g) icing sugar	
3–4 leaves gelatine (or 1 tablespoon powdered gelatine)	

Put the hazelnuts on a baking sheet and toast them in the oven at Gas Mark 6 (400°F) until the skins rub off easily. Rub off the skins with a clean cloth and grind the nuts. Mix together the ground hazelnuts, sugar and flour and rub in the butter. Work into a smooth dough, pat into a round and chill for about 30 minutes.

Divide the dough into three equal portions. Roll or press each portion into a round approximately 9 inches in diameter. Prick each round with a fork and then set them on buttered and floured baking sheets. Bake at Gas Mark 5 (375°F) for about 25 minutes. Remove carefully and set to cool on a rack.

Sprinkle the strawberries with the sugar and leave to stand for about 15 minutes. Sieve the strawberries or reduce to a purée in a blender. Dissolve the gelatine in 3–4 tablespoons of hot water, cool slightly and stir into the strawberry purée. Whisk the cream until thick and fold into the strawberry purée. Chill.

Trim the rounds of pastry if necessary and sandwich together with the strawberry filling just as it is on the point of setting. Dust over the top with icing sugar. Serve as soon as possible after the rounds have been assembled.

Chestnut gâteau I
(no baking required)

FOR THE BASE

1 lb (450g) chestnuts weighed in their skins	3½ oz (100g) icing sugar
	1 teaspoon vanilla sugar
2½ oz (70g) butter	a good dash of rum

FOR THE TOPPING

3½ oz (100g) bitter chocolate	1 oz (30g) butter

There are easier ways of preparing the chestnuts than the one I am advocating – like slitting the chestnuts across and putting them first into a hot oven – but they do not work quite as well for this particular recipe. Cooked whole chestnuts sold in tins are not suitable as they have usually absorbed too much water, and tinned chestnut purée is too soft. To get the right firm consistency the chestnuts should be boiled whole and without previously slitting the skins.

Put the chestnuts into a large saucepan, cover with plenty of cold water, bring to the boil and cook until the chestnuts are soft. This usually takes about 30–40 minutes, depending on size, and you will simply have to test them to see if they are done. Just fish out one of the chestnuts with a slotted spoon and plunge a sharp pointed knife through the hard outer skin. If it goes smoothly through the chestnut flesh, they are done. Keep the water simmering gently as you fish out two or three chestnuts at a time and peel off the skins, then push the chestnuts through a sieve or a potato ricer while they are still hot. Proceed until all the chestnuts have been peeled and sieved (do not use a food processor for mashing up the chestnuts – it does not work as well as sieving them or using a potato ricer).

Cream together the butter and sugar until light and fluffy, beat in the vanilla sugar and the rum and then mix in the sieved chestnuts – it may at first seem quite a lot of chestnuts for the amount of butter, but it will all work into a rather smooth paste. Line a 7-inch cake tin – preferably one with a spring clip – with greaseproof paper (this is a case where greaseproof paper is better than kitchen foil). Press the chestnut mixture into the tin, level the top and cover with a plate which should just fit the inside of the tin. Place a weight on top and set to chill overnight.

On the next day lift out the cake and peel off the greaseproof paper. Set the cake on a plate and prepare the topping. Break the chocolate into small pieces, put them into a bowl and set to melt either over steam or in a warm oven. Soften the butter a little, then beat the softened butter into the melted but not hot chocolate. Smooth over the cake and leave to set. Serve cut into thin slices – with sweetened whipped cream if you like, though it is excellent on its own.

Chestnut gâteau II

FOR THE CAKE

6 eggs
5 oz (140g) icing sugar
5 oz (140g) cooked sieved chestnuts

2½ oz (70g) fine breadcrumbs
butter and fine breadcrumbs for the cake tin

FILLING

9 fl oz (250ml) cream
2 tablespoons icing sugar

4 oz (110g) cooked sieved chestnuts

icing sugar and vanilla sugar for the top

Preheat the oven to Gas Mark 4 (350°F). Butter a 10-inch spring-clip cake tin and dust lightly with fine breadcrumbs. Separate the egg yolks and whites. Whisk together the yolks and icing sugar until very thick and fluffy. Gently fold in the sieved chestnuts. Whisk the egg whites until stiff and fold into the mixture, alternately with the breadcrumbs. Bake for ¾–1 hour. Leave to cool for a little while in the tin, then set to cool on a rack.

For the filling, whisk the cream until it holds a soft peak. Gently whisk in the sugar and then fold in the sieved chestnuts.

Cut through the cake and spread the filling between the two

layers. Dust the top with icing sugar to which a little vanilla sugar has been added.

Walnut gâteau

FOR THE CAKE

6 eggs

2 tablespoons rum

1½ oz (40g) fine
  breadcrumbs

5 oz (140g) icing sugar, sifted

5 oz (140g) ground walnuts

butter and ground walnuts
  for the cake tin

FOR THE BUTTER CREAM

3 egg yolks

1 scant teaspoon cornflour

6 fl oz (170ml) cream

5 oz (140g) butter

4 oz (110g) icing sugar

½ oz (15g) vanilla sugar

FOR THE TOPPING

about 3 tablespoons
  redcurrant jelly

lemon juice

7 oz (200g) icing sugar

walnut halves for decoration

Preheat the oven to Gas Mark 4 (350°F). Butter a 9- or 10-inch spring-clip cake tin and dust with ground walnuts.

Separate the egg yolks and whites. Add the rum to the breadcrumbs and leave to stand while whisking together the egg yolks and sugar until very thick and creamy. Gently beat in the softened breadcrumbs. Whisk the egg whites until stiff, then fold them into the yolks mixture, alternately with the ground walnuts. Put the mixture into the prepared cake tin and bake for about 45–50 minutes.

Test carefully before turning off the oven. Leave the cake to cool in the tin for about 5 minutes, then turn it out on to a rack. Leave to cool very gradually – overnight if possible. As with all rich cakes, it is best to leave the filling and icing until the next day. And it is also best to turn the cake upside down so that the icing is spread over the perfectly smooth part of the cake.

To prepare the butter cream filling, whisk the egg yolks, cornflour and cream over steam until the mixture is very thick. Cream together the butter, sugar and vanilla sugar until fluffy, then beat in the egg yolk mixture by the teaspoonful. The final consistency should be that of very thick mayonnaise.

Cut the cake into two or three parts and sandwich them together with the butter cream. (I prefer cutting the cake into two layers only, but this is a matter of personal taste.)

Heat the redcurrant jelly and spread over the top and sides of the cake. Leave to dry a little.

Beat enough lemon juice into the sifted icing sugar to give a thick paste and spread this over the top and sides of the cake. When the icing is just beginning to set, decorate the top of the cake with halved walnuts.

Coffee gâteau

No cooking is required for this delectable gâteau.

boudoir biscuits
5 oz (140g) butter
5 oz (140g) icing sugar
3–4 egg yolks
1 teaspoon vanilla sugar
2 tablespoons strong black
  coffee
1 small carton (5 fl oz/140ml)
  single cream
1 tablespoon strong black
  coffee
dash of rum
whipped cream and finely
  ground coffee beans for
  decoration

The size of boudoir biscuits varies a little according to the brand. This does not matter as long as you aim for a square-shaped gâteau, but it is impossible to give the exact number of biscuits required.

Cream together the butter and the icing sugar until very light and fluffy. Gradually beat in the egg yolks, the vanilla sugar and the coffee.

Tip the single cream into a soup plate and add the tablespoon of coffee and a dash of rum. Pull some boudoir biscuits quickly through the cream – one by one so that they do not get soggy – and arrange them side by side on a dish so that they form a square. Spread a little of the butter cream over them, then cover with more boudoir biscuits, also pulled through the coffee cream in the soup plate, laying them at right angles across the first layer. Continue until all the butter cream has been used up. Cover the resulting 'brick' lightly with foil and set it to chill in a cold place overnight.

Just before serving, mask the gâteau with whipped, lightly sweetened cream and sprinkle with very finely ground coffee beans.

Truffle gâteau

FOR THE CAKE

3 eggs

4½ oz (125g) butter

4½ oz (125g) icing sugar

3½ oz (100g) plain chocolate, grated

5½ oz (150g) flour

1 teaspoon baking powder

4½ fl oz (125ml) cold milk

butter and flour for the cake tin

FOR THE FILLING

9 oz (250g) best plain chocolate

9 fl oz (250ml) cream

3½ oz (100g) butter

a little unsweetened cocoa powder

Preheat the oven to Gas Mark 5 (375°F). Butter and flour a 9- or 10-inch spring-clip cake tin (in the latter case you will get a slightly shallower cake, but as it is a very rich cake, you may find this preferable). Separate the egg yolks and whites. Cream the butter and sugar until very light and fluffy, then beat in the egg yolks one by one. Gradually add the finely grated chocolate and then the flour sifted together with the baking powder, alternately with the milk. Whisk the egg whites until stiff and fold very carefully into the mixture. Bake for about 50–60 minutes (test the cake before removing from oven). Carefully invert the cake on to a rack and leave to cool. Leave overnight before filling.

For the filling, grate the chocolate or break it into small lumps. Put the cream, the chocolate and the butter into a small, thick saucepan and heat very gently over a low flame, stirring all the time, until the chocolate has melted. As soon as this happens, remove the saucepan from the heat and pour the mixture into a bowl to cool. Do not stir any more. When the mixture is quite cold – you can accelerate this by putting the bowl into the refrigerator, but I prefer to let it cool more gradually – whisk the mixture until it will stand up in soft peaks.

The colour of the chocolate will change as you whisk the mixture – it will get much lighter – and this is exactly as it should be. Cut through the cake once – or twice if you have used a 9-inch tin – and sandwich together with the chocolate cream filling, reserving some for the top and sides of the cake. Spread the remaining mixture over the top and sides and dust very lightly with a little unsweetened cocoa. Keep the gâteau in a cold place before serving.

Apple cake

FOR THE PASTRY
5 oz (140g) flour
pinch of salt
5 oz (140g) butter
1 egg yolk

2 tablespoons cream
butter and flour for the
    baking sheet

FOR THE TOPPING
2–3 cooking apples
a good dash of rum
2 tablespoons icing sugar
1 teaspoon vanilla sugar

2 eggs
2½ oz (70g) icing or caster
    sugar
2½ oz (70g) ground almonds

Preheat the oven to Gas Mark 4 (350°F). Butter and flour a baking tin measuring about 7×11 inches. Sift together the flour and salt, cut in the butter and work quickly to a smooth paste with the egg yolk and cream. Press the pastry into the baking sheet – no need to roll it out, just press it out with your fingers.

173

Peel, score and slice the apples and spread them over the pastry. Sprinkle with rum and the 2 tablespoons of icing sugar and vanilla sugar. Separate the egg yolks and whites. Whisk the yolks with the 2½ oz icing or caster sugar until thick and fluffy, then whisk the egg whites until stiff. Fold the egg whites into the egg yolks, alternately with the ground almonds. Spread over the apples, masking them completely. Bake for 35–45 minutes. Leave to cool in the tin, but cut into slices while still warm. It is one of those cakes which almost taste best when served straight from the tin!

Dark cherry cake

5 oz (140g) chocolate
5 oz (140g) butter
5 oz (140g) icing or caster
  sugar
4 eggs

5 oz (140g) flour
black cherries
butter and flour for the cake
  tin

Preheat the oven to Gas Mark 4 (350°F). Break the chocolate into small pieces and set it to melt either over steam or in the oven. Butter and flour a square or rectangular cake tin.

Cream the butter with the sugar until light and fluffy. Separate the egg whites from the yolks, then beat the yolks into the butter mixture, one by one. Add the melted but not hot chocolate, then fold in the flour alternately with the stiffly beaten egg whites. Spread the mixture lightly over the cake tin, then stud the top with cherries. Do not press them down, they will sink into the cake of their own accord (whether or not you stone the cherries is a matter for personal preference, but if the cherries are very juicy it is best to leave them whole). Bake for about 40–45 minutes. Leave to cool in the tin and cut into slices when cold.

Walnut layer cake

FOR THE CAKE
7½ oz (210g) flour
5 oz (140g) caster or icing
  sugar
5 oz (140g) ground walnuts

5 oz (140g) butter
butter and flour for the
  baking sheet

FOR THE FILLING
½ pint (275ml) cream
1 lightly heaped tablespoon
  vanilla sugar

Mix together the flour, sugar and ground walnuts, then cut the butter into this quickly and work to a smooth paste. Divide the mixture into four equal-sized pieces. Roll out each piece into a round or a square – the shape does not really matter, all that matters is that the pieces should be of the same size. (I usually use the bottom of a spring-clip cake tin as a guide.) Bake the pastry on a well-buttered and floured baking sheet at Gas Mark 5 (375°F) until deep golden brown – about 12–15 minutes. (If you have a large baking sheet, set them side by side and bake two at a time.) As soon as the pastry comes out of the oven, loosen it carefully with a spatula or a palette knife. When the rounds (or squares) have cooled a little, set them carefully on a rack to cool completely. This is the only tricky part of the whole operation – the pastry is rather fragile and has to be handled rather carefully.

While the pastry is cooling, whip the cream until just stiff, then whisk in the vanilla sugar. Sandwich the pastry rounds (or squares) together with the whipped cream, leaving the top bare. Put the cake into the refrigerator overnight. Dust the top lightly with icing sugar before serving.

Rich chocolate cake

FOR THE CAKE

5½ oz (150g) plain or bitter
   chocolate
dash of rum
3½ oz (100g) butter
5½ oz (150g) icing sugar

1 flat teaspoon vanilla sugar
4 eggs
5½ oz (150g) ground walnuts
butter and flour for the cake
   tin

FOR THE ICING

2 heaped tablespoons good
   apricot jam
4 oz (120g) plain or bitter
   chocolate

4 oz (120g) caster sugar
3 fl oz (75ml) water
a few drops of olive oil

Butter and flour a 9- or 10-inch spring-clip cake tin. Preheat the
oven to Gas Mark 4½ (about 360°F).

Break the chocolate into small pieces, add a dash of rum and
leave the chocolate to soften over steam or in the oven. Cream
the butter with the sugar until very light and fluffy. Beat in the
vanilla sugar. Separate the egg whites and yolks. Beat the yolks,
one by one, into the creamed butter, then beat in the softened
but not hot chocolate. Whisk the whites until stiff and fold into
the mixture, alternately with the ground walnuts.

Bake for about 50–60 minutes. Test carefully before
removing from the oven. Leave to cool a little before removing
the cake from the tin. Set to cool on a rack. If possible, leave
the cake overnight before icing it. It is iced 'upside down', the
absolutely flat bottom of the cake becoming the top.

Spread the top and sides of the cake with warmed, sieved
apricot jam and leave to dry a little.

Break the chocolate for the icing into small pieces and set
them to melt over steam or in a warm oven. Dissolve the sugar

in the water and cook to 'small thread' stage. Remove from the fire and leave to cool a little. Stir the lukewarm sugar into the melted chocolate and add one or two drops – no more – of olive oil. Spread the icing quickly over the cake, using a palette knife dipped into hot water. Leave to set.

My favourite aunt's favourite chocolate cake

This makes a lovely moist, though not very high, cake. Excellent as it is, but better still if covered with chocolate icing as for the rich chocolate cake (see above).

6 eggs
5 oz (140g) icing sugar
juice and grated rind of ½ lemon
3½ oz (100g) grated chocolate

2½ oz (70g) ground unblanched almonds
2 oz (50g) fine breadcrumbs moistened with rum
butter and flour for the cake tin

Preheat the oven to Gas Mark 5 (375°F). Butter and flour a 9- or 10-inch spring-clip cake tin.

Separate the egg yolks and whites. Whisk the yolks with the sugar and lemon juice until very thick and creamy. Whisk the whites until stiff. Fold the whites into the yolks, alternately with the grated chocolate, almonds and breadcrumbs. Finally fold in the grated lemon rind. Bake for 50–60 minutes. Allow to cool for a little while in the tin, then remove carefully and set on a rack to finish cooling.

Lore's cake

More of a rich and delectable pudding than a cake, this is even better on the day after which it was baked.

6 eggs	grated chocolate
6½ oz (180g) butter	butter and flour for the cake
6½ oz (180g) icing sugar	tin
dash of rum	
6½ oz (180g) plain or bitter chocolate, melted	

Butter and flour a 10-inch spring-clip cake tin. Preheat the oven to Gas Mark 1 (275°F).

Separate the egg yolks and whites. Cream the butter and sugar until light and fluffy, then beat in the egg yolks, one by one, creaming well after each addition. Beat in the rum and the melted but not hot chocolate. Whisk the egg whites until stiff, then fold into the egg/chocolate mixture. Put a third of the mixture into the prepared cake tin and bake for about 35 minutes – the cake will still be slightly moist inside. Carefully remove the spring clip from the tin, but leave the cake to sit on the base. Set to cool and then mask the top and sides completely with the remaining chocolate mixture. Sprinkle with grated chocolate. Do not attempt to remove the cake from the base – just set it on a larger plate or dish and serve it from there.

Hungarian chocolate cake

FOR THE CAKE
6 eggs
3½ oz (100g) plain or bitter
  chocolate
3 tablespoons water
2 oz (60g) butter
5 oz (140g) icing sugar

1 teaspoon vanilla sugar
5 oz (140g) ground
  unblanched almonds
butter and flour for the cake
  tin

FOR THE FILLING
2 oz (60g) unblanched
  almonds
5 oz (140g) plain or bitter
  chocolate
4 tablespoons water

1 tablespoon icing sugar
5 oz (140g) butter
1 heaped teaspoon vanilla
  sugar
2 egg yolks

Preheat the oven to Gas Mark 4½ (about 360°F). Butter and flour a 10-inch cake tin with a spring-clip bottom.

Separate the yolks and whites of five of the eggs. Break the chocolate into small pieces and put them into a small, thick saucepan with the water. Stir over a low flame until the chocolate has melted. Remove the pan from the heat and leave to cool.

Cream together the butter, sugar and vanilla sugar until very light and fluffy, then beat in the five egg yolks, one by one. Cream well after each addition. Beat in the cooled chocolate and the sixth egg. Whisk the five egg whites until stiff, fold into the mixture, alternately with the ground almonds. Put the mixture into the prepared cake tin and bake for 50–60 minutes. Test the cake before taking it out of the oven, and leave it to cool a little in the tin before turning it out – upside-down – on a rack to cool completely.

179

For the filling, put the almonds on a baking sheet and set them to brown lightly in the oven. The oven temperature does not matter greatly, as long as you watch the almonds and do not let them burn. Grind the almonds. Break the chocolate into small pieces, put them into a thick saucepan, add the water and the sugar and stir over a low flame until the chocolate has dissolved completely. Cook very gently until the mixture has thickened slightly, then remove it from the heat and leave to cool. Cream the butter with the vanilla sugar until thick and fluffy, then beat in the cooled chocolate and the egg yolks. Finally, stir in the ground toasted almonds.

Cut through the cake once and fill it with half the chocolate cream. Spread remaining cream over top and sides. You can also reserve some of the ground almonds and sprinkle them over the top and sides of the cake – it does not alter the taste, only the appearance!

Fruit and walnut roulade

4 eggs
3 oz (80g) icing or caster
  sugar
1½ oz (30g) flour
1½ oz (30g) ground walnuts
1–2 bananas

a little rum
10 fl oz (275ml) cream
1 flat tablespoon vanilla sugar
butter and flour for the
  baking sheet

Line a baking sheet (measuring approximately 12×8 inches) with buttered foil or buttered greaseproof paper and dust lightly with flour. Preheat the oven to Gas Mark 5 (375°F).

Whisk together the eggs and sugar until very thick and creamy and pale in colour. Lightly fold in the flour and ground walnuts. Spread the mixture over the baking sheet and bake for about 20 minutes.

Sprinkle a piece of clean kitchen paper with flour and turn the pastry on to this. Peel off the foil or greaseproof paper while the pastry is still hot. Lightly roll up the pastry – it is more a case of folding over than of rolling up – and leave to cool. Slice the banana thinly and sprinkle with a little rum. Whisk the cream until stiff, lightly whisk in the vanilla sugar.

When the pastry has cooled, trim off the edges if necessary and spread with the whipped cream. Arrange the banana slices on top and fold up very lightly. Do not roll up as for Swiss roll, just fold it over so that the cream filling is in the centre. Wrap up the roll in kitchen foil – folded side of pastry underneath – and chill for at least half an hour before slicing it, longer if possible. You could spread a little extra whipped cream over the top, if you wished, but I find that a light dusting of icing sugar is all that is required. Raspberries or strawberries – sprinkled with Kirsch or Framboise – instead of bananas are also delicious as filling.

Walnut roulade

FOR THE ROULADE

2 tablespoons milk	6 oz (170g) butter
1 oz (25g) fresh yeast	3 egg yolks, lightly beaten
1 teaspoon sugar	butter and flour for the
6 oz (170g) strong flour	baking sheet

FOR THE FILLING

5 oz (170g) shelled walnuts	6 oz (170g) icing sugar
3 egg whites	1 teaspoon vanilla sugar

Heat the milk to lukewarm. Cream the yeast with the sugar in a cup, then stir in the lukewarm milk. Sprinkle about a teaspoon of the flour over the top and set it to 'prove' in a warm place.

Meanwhile, sift the flour into a bowl, cut the butter into the flour and then crumble it with your fingers until the mixture has the consistency of fine breadcrumbs. When the yeast starts to bubble, add it to the flour, together with the lightly beaten egg yolks. Work the mixture to a paste, pat it into a round and slip the mixture into a large plastic bag. Fasten the top and put the pastry into the refrigerator for 1–2 hours. (I know I should advocate that the inside of the bag be lightly oiled, but I find that this is not really necessary – just dust a little flour over the pastry to prevent it from sticking to the bag.)

While the pastry is in the refrigerator, grind the walnuts finely or crush them with a rolling pin between sheets of kitchen foil or greaseproof paper (an electric coffee mill makes a fine job of this part of the operation). Butter and flour a large baking sheet or roasting tin. Preheat the oven to Gas Mark 6 (400°F). Roll out the pastry on a well–floured pastry board (knead it briefly before rolling out) into a rectangle of about ⅛-inch thickness. Whisk the egg whites until stiff, gradually add the icing and the vanilla sugar and whisk until smooth, then fold in the ground walnuts. Spread this mixture over the pastry to within about ½ inch of the edges, then roll up the pastry lightly – rather like a Swiss roll. Slide it on to the baking sheet or into the roasting tin – 'pastry seam' side underneath – and gently bend the roll into a horseshoe as it slides into the tin. Put it into the oven leaving the oven door very slightly open for the first 10 minutes. After that close the oven door gently and leave the roulade to bake for another 20–25 minutes, until it is a beautiful brown. Leave to cool in the tin for a little while, then slide it out, dust with a little vanilla sugar and slice when cold.

Chocolate roulade

FOR THE ROULADE

6 egg yolks

5 slightly heaped tablespoons
 caster or icing sugar

4 slightly heaped tablespoons
 cocoa

3 egg whites

butter and flour for the
 baking sheet

FOR THE FILLING

½ pint (275ml) cream

1 packet vanilla sugar

1 heaped tablespoon icing
 sugar

Preheat the oven to Gas Mark 5 (375°F). Line a Swiss roll tin or other suitable baking sheet with greaseproof paper. Brush the paper with softened butter and dust lightly with flour.

Whisk together the egg yolks and the sugar until thick and creamy and almost white. Stir in 3 tablespoons cocoa. Whisk the egg whites until stiff and fold lightly into the mixture, alternately with the remaining cocoa.

Spread the mixture over the prepared baking sheet and bake for about 10 minutes – until the top is slightly firm to the touch. Wring out a tea towel in cold water and spread it on to a kitchen table (or dust the table lightly with flour). Turn out the pastry very carefully and remove the greaseproof paper. Roll up the pastry in the tea towel – or in kitchen paper dusted with flour – and allow it to get cold.

Whisk the cream until thick, add the vanilla sugar and the icing sugar and whisk again very lightly. Spread this over the cooled pastry and roll up again very lightly. Cut into thick slices for serving.

Styrian apple tart

FOR THE PASTRY

9 oz (250g) flour
1 oz (25g) icing sugar
pinch of salt
4½ oz (125g) butter

1 egg
2 tablespoons milk
butter and flour for the
    pie dish

FOR THE TOPPING

about 1 lb (450g) eating
    apples
2 eggs
1 oz (25g) icing or caster
    sugar

3 fl oz (85ml) milk
4 fl oz (120ml) cream
1 flat teaspoon vanilla sugar
dash of rum

Sift the flour with the sugar and a pinch of salt on to a pastry board. Cut the butter into the flour and then work it quickly to a paste with the egg and the milk. Pat into a round and leave it covered in a cool place for about ½ hour.

Meanwhile peel, core, halve and then slice the apples very thinly. A mandoline cutter is excellent for this, and so is the cutting attachment of a food processor.

Preheat the oven to Gas Mark 4½ (about 360°F). Butter and lightly flour a large pie dish, ideally one from which the apple tart can be served. Line the dish with pastry – no need to roll out the pastry first, just press it out with your knuckles, but make sure that the pastry is not too thick where the bottom and sides of the pie dish join. Prick over the base with a fork and fill the dish with overlapping slices of apple.

Whisk together the eggs and sugar until fluffy, then whisk in the milk, cream and vanilla sugar. Add a good dash of rum. Pour this mixture over the apples and bake until golden brown on top. It is at its most delicious when served just slightly warm.

184

Cherry tart

FOR THE PASTRY

7 oz (200g) flour

2 oz (55g) icing sugar

3½ oz (90g) butter

1 egg

butter and flour for the tin

a little egg white

FOR THE TOPPING

¾ lb (340g) black or Morello cherries

3 eggs

2 oz (55g) icing or caster sugar

1 teaspoon vanilla sugar

3 tablespoons sour cream

2 oz (55g) finely chopped almonds

ground almonds or biscuit crumbs

Sift together the flour and icing sugar. Cut the butter into the mixture and quickly work to a paste with the egg. Shape into a ball and chill for about half an hour.

Butter and flour a large flan case. I use a fluted ovenproof dish, measuring 9½ inches in diameter and about 2 inches high, from which the cherry tart can be served. Line the dish with pastry – no need to roll it out, just press it out with your fingers, but make sure that the pastry is not too thick where the bottom and sides of the flan case join. Prick all over the pastry with a fork and then brush it lightly with egg white. Bake at Gas Mark 5 (375°F) until lightly tinged with colour – about 10–12 minutes.

Stone the cherries. Separate the egg yolks and whites. Whisk the egg yolks with the sugar and vanilla sugar until very thick and fluffy, then whisk in the sour cream. Whisk the egg whites until stiff, then fold them into the egg yolk mixture, alternately with the chopped almonds. Cover the flan case with the stoned cherries and then pile the egg mixture on top. Sprinkle with ground almonds or fine biscuit crumbs and bake at Gas Mark 4 (350°F) until nicely browned on top – about 30–40 minutes.

Greengage tart

FOR THE PASTRY

7 oz (200g) flour
2 oz (60g) icing sugar
3½ oz (100g) butter

1 egg
butter and flour for the flan
    case

FOR THE TOPPING

1 scant teaspoon flour
9 fl oz (250ml) milk
2 eggs
3½ oz (100g) icing sugar
1 teaspoon vanilla sugar

apricot jam
about 1 lb (450g) greengages
1 tablespoon ground
    almonds

Mix together the flour and sugar, crumble the butter into this and work to a paste with the egg. Cover and leave while preparing the topping. For this, slake the flour with a little of the milk, whisk in the eggs. Heat the remaining milk with the sugar and vanilla sugar and pour on to the egg mixture, stirring all the time. Return the mixture to the stove and cook very gently over low heat, still stirring all the time, until thickened. (I could now advocate the use of a double boiler, but this is not really necessary and only prolongs the procedure – just go gently so that the mixture does not burn or curdle.) Remove the mixture from the heat and leave to cool, stirring from time to time.

Butter and flour a fairly large flan case – I use a fluted ovenproof dish measuring about 9½ inches in diameter and about 2 inches high, from which the greengage tart can also be served. Line the bottom and sides of the case with pastry – no need to roll it, just press it out with the knuckles of your hands, but make sure that the pastry is not too thick where the bottom and sides of the case join. Prick all over with a fork. Spread

186

with apricot jam and if you happen to have a little leftover egg white (which I always seem to have), spread the pastry first with this and then with the apricot jam. Cover with stoned and halved greengages, cut side down. Bake at Gas Mark 5 (375°F) for 15–20 minutes until the sides are just tinged with colour and the greengages appear to have a sort of 'glazed' look, then pour the egg cream over them. Sprinkle with ground almonds and bake for another 30–40 minutes at Gas Mark 4 (350°F). Leave to cool before serving.

Redcurrant meringue

FOR THE PASTRY

7 oz (200g) flour
3 oz (85g) caster sugar
grated rind and juice of ½
　lemon

5 oz (140g) butter
2 large egg yolks
butter and flour for the
　baking sheet

FOR THE TOPPING

¾ lb (350g) redcurrants
2 large egg whites

4 oz (110g) caster sugar

Mix together the flour, sugar and grated lemon rind. Cut or crumble the butter into the dry ingredients. Add the egg yolks and lemon juice and work to a smooth dough, handling it as little as possible. Butter and flour a baking sheet – a Swiss roll tin measuring about 9×12 inches will do nicely – and press out the dough with your fingers straight on to the baking sheet. Chill for at least 30 minutes.

Preheat the oven to Gas Mark 5 (375°F). Prick the pastry all over with a fork and bake until just golden brown. This usually takes about 15–20 minutes – just long enough to remove the stems from the redcurrants. Take the pastry out of the oven and lower the oven heat to Gas Mark 1 (275°F) – leave open the oven door to reduce the heat a little more quickly.

Whisk the egg whites until stiff, then whisk in the sugar gradually until the mixture is very smooth and glossy. Spread the redcurrants over the top of the pastry, juice and all. Mask them completely with the meringue and return the whole thing to the oven until the meringue has dried out and is just lightly tinged with colour. If the oven has not cooled down sufficiently, leave the oven door open for a little while. Mark the pastry into slices while still warm.

Raspberry meringue tart

3½ oz (100g) marzipan
3½ oz (100g) butter
5 oz (140g) flour
1 egg yolk
3 egg whites

5½ oz (150g) caster sugar
about 1 lb (450g) raspberries
butter and flour for the cake tin

Put the marzipan (shop-bought will do excellently provided it is a good brand) into the refrigerator to harden. Rub the butter into the flour, then coarsely grate the marzipan into this – or cut it up into small pieces. Quickly work in the egg yolk, handling the mixture as little as possible.

Butter and flour a 10-inch spring-clip cake tin or flan case. Press out the pastry to line the bottom and sides of the tin – no need to roll out the pastry, just gently press it out with your fingers – then prick it all over with a fork and chill for 30 minutes.

Preheat the oven to Gas Mark 4 (350°F). Bake the pastry for about 25–30 minutes, until golden brown. Take out of the oven, but leave in the tin and reduce the oven heat to Gas Mark 1 (275°F). Let the pastry cool a little while whisking the egg whites until stiff, then whisk in the caster sugar gradually. The mixture should be very smooth and glossy. Cover the pastry base thickly with the raspberries and mask completely with the meringue mixture. Bake the tart until the top is just lightly tinged with colour – about 10 minutes.

Styrian yeast cake
(makes two cakes)

FOR THE DOUGH

13 fl oz (375ml) milk
½ oz (12g) fresh yeast
1½ oz (40g) sugar
9 oz (250g) flour
pinch salt
1 teaspoon vanilla sugar

grated lemon rind
2 egg yolks
4½ oz (120g) melted butter
butter and flour for the
    cake tins

FOR THE TOPPING

18 oz (500g) cottage or
    cream cheese
12 fl oz (330ml) fresh or sour
    cream
1 egg

7 oz (200g) caster sugar
1 teaspoon vanilla sugar
a little extra cream
2 heaped tablespoons
    granulated sugar

Preheat the oven to Gas Mark 7 (425°F). Heat the milk to lukewarm. Cream the yeast with a heaped teaspoon of the sugar and the same amount of flour in a cup. Stir in enough milk to fill the cup to about two-thirds. Set in a warm place to prove. Sift together the flour, salt, remaining sugar and vanilla sugar into a bowl. Add the lemon rind. When the yeast has risen to the top of the cup, add it to the flour, together with the remaining milk and the egg yolks. Beat well to blend, then beat in the melted but not hot butter. If using an electric beater, do not use the dough hook attachment but the egg whisk as the dough is very soft. Beat the mixture until it is smooth and starts to blister slightly. Cover with a cloth and set to rise in a warm place until almost doubled in size – about 45 minutes.

Meanwhile prepare the topping. If using cottage cheese, press it through a sieve to get rid of any lumps. Gradually beat in the cream and the egg, caster sugar and vanilla sugar. If you are using fresh cream, you may like to add a little lemon juice. Cover and set aside.

When the dough has almost doubled in size, beat it again lightly, then pour it into two buttered and floured 9- or 10-inch cake tins. Cover and set to rise again in a warm place for about 30 minutes.

Divide the cream cheese mixture equally between the two cake tins. As the dough is very soft – practically the consistency of a batter – it is not possible to spread the mixture, just divide it over the top. It will sink in almost immediately, with the dough bubbling over the top, and that is exactly as it should be. Bake for 35–40 minutes by which time the cakes will be golden brown on top but not quite baked through. Quickly pour a little cream over the top of each cake and sprinkle with the granulated sugar. Lower the oven heat to Gas Mark 6 (400°F) and return the cakes to the oven. Bake for another 10–15 minutes.

Icecreams and sorbets

One of my best buys ever was a small electric icecream maker which I brought back from Italy. It cost me about £9 at the time and there was nothing like it available in this country then. Neat, compact and very efficient, it fitted into the freezing compartment of my refrigerator like the proverbial glove and over the years it must have made gallons of icecream. It is still going strong, and although there are now similar – and possibly improved – versions on the market here. I would not change it for anything in the world. Pour in the mixture, close the lid and switch on – and the machine will do the rest. It will even switch off when the icecream is ready. I commend it – or a similar model – to anyone wanting to make their own icecreams and sorbets.

The joy about making icecreams and sorbets is that nothing can really go wrong – as long as you remember that anything that is frozen should be slightly more flavoured as freezing tends to dull the flavour a little. Also, if you intend making a lot of fruit sorbets it is a good idea to keep a stock of sugar syrup in the refrigerator and simply allow equal quantities of fruit pulp and sugar syrup, plus any flavouring such as lemon juice or a sprinkling of vanilla sugar. No need even to look up a recipe . . .

Sugar syrup for home-made ices

1 lb (450g) caster sugar   ¾ pint (425ml) water

Dissolve the sugar in the water over low heat. Bring to the boil and then simmer for about 4–5 minutes. Leave to cool, bottle and store in the refrigerator.

Apricot icecream

1½ lb (675g) ripe apricots   9 fl oz (250ml) cream
4–5 oz (110–140g) icing sugar   2 egg whites
juice of ½ lemon

Halve and stone the apricots. Barely cover them with water then simmer them gently until they are soft. Purée the apricots, then stir in the lemon juice and the sugar. The quantity of sugar depends on the ripeness of the apricots and you will simply have to taste the purée, but remember that a little of the sweetness is lost in freezing. Leave to cool. Set the refrigerator control at maximum.

Whisk the cream until stiff, then whisk the egg whites until stiff in a separate bowl. Fold the egg whites and whipped cream lightly into the apricot purée. Remove the partitions from the icecube tray. Pile the mixture into the tray, cover lightly with foil and set to freeze. Stirring should not be necessary.

Morello cherry icecream

1 lb (450g) Morello cherries
juice of 1 lemon
1 liqueur glass of Kirsch

sugar syrup (see page 192)
small pinch of cinnamon
½ pint (275ml) cream

Stone the cherries and crush a small handful of the stones. Put the stones into a muslin bag and add them to the cherries. Add the lemon juice and the Kirsch, cover and leave to stand in a cool place for about an hour. Remove the muslin bag with the stones and put the cherries – juice and all – through the blender or food processor (or sieve them). Measure the resulting purée and add the same amount of sugar syrup and a small pinch of cinnamon. Whisk the cream until stiff and fold into the purée. Put the mixture into the icecube tray – having previously removed the partitions and set the control at maximum. Cover with foil and set the mixture to freeze. It should not require any stirring while it freezes, but check and, if necessary, stir gently with a fork, drawing in the icecream from the sides where it will freeze first.

If you have an icecream maker you can either add the unwhipped cream to the purée, put it into the machine and let the machine do the work or – for an even smoother finish – put the fruit purée into the machine, turn it on and when the purée is half-frozen whip the cream to the same consistency. Fold it into the fruit purée, return the machine to the refrigerator and turn it on again to complete freezing.

Raspberry icecream

½ lb (225g) raspberries   1 teaspoon vanilla sugar
3 tablespoons sugar   ½ pint (275ml) cream

Turn the refrigerator control to maximum. Sprinkle the sugar and the vanilla sugar over the raspberries and leave to stand until the juices start to run. Sieve the raspberries – or use a food processor or liquidizer first and then sieve the raspberries to dispose of the pips. Whisk the cream until it stands in soft peaks and fold into the raspberry purée. Pour the mixture into the icecube tray (or trays) having first removed the partitions. Cover lightly with foil and set to freeze. Stirring should not be necessary, but check during the freezing time.

If you have an icecream machine, just add the cream – without whipping it first – to the raspberry purée and stir, then put the mixture into the machine and switch on – the machine will do the rest.

Hazelnut icecream

3 oz (85g) hazelnuts   1 teaspoon vanilla sugar
2 eggs   ½ pint (275ml) cream
2 oz (55g) icing sugar

Set the refrigerator control to maximum. Put the hazelnuts on a baking sheet and leave to brown at Gas Mark 6 (400°F) until the skins rub off easily. Grind the hazelnuts very finely – an electric foodmill or food processor is ideal as it will reduce the hazelnuts to a fine powder. Whisk the eggs with the sugar and vanilla sugar over steam until light and frothy, remove from steam and whisk until cool – set the bowl over crushed ice to accelerate this. Pour the mixture into the icecream maker, put it into the freezing compartment of the refrigerator and turn it on. When the mixture is half-frozen, whisk the cream to the same consistency as the half-frozen mixture and fold it in, together with the ground hazelnuts. Return the machine to the refrigerator to complete freezing.

If not using an icecream maker, put the mixture into the icecube tray, having removed the partitions, and when it is beginning to 'take' tip it into a bowl, then fold in the cream, whipped to the same consistency, and the hazelnuts. Return to the tray, cover with foil and put into freezing compartment to complete.

Iced chestnut mousse

8¾ oz (250g) tinned   1 tablespoon rum
  sweetened chestnut purée   5 fl oz (140ml) cream

Set the refrigerator control to maximum. Tip the chestnut purée into a bowl, add the rum and stir to mix. (I use a French brand of chestnut purée which is not only sweetened but also lightly scented with vanilla.)

Whisk the cream until stiff and about the same consistency as that of the chestnut purée. Fold the whipped cream into the chestnut purée and taste it – the sweetness of the various brands of chestnut purée varies a little, but if the mixture tastes absolutely marvellous and you want to go on eating it, it's about right. It should be slightly too sweet, in fact, as some of the sweetness is lost in the freezing. If it tastes very much too sweet, stir in a little cream – or even top of the milk.

Take the partitions from the icecube tray and tip the mixture into it. Cover lightly with foil and put it into the icecube compartment of the refrigerator. If the compartment is very large and you have an icecream *bombe* mould, you can use this instead of the icecube tray. The mixture will not quite freeze, merely set into the most delicious creamy mousse. On one occasion I put the mixtue – absentmindedly, I admit – into my icecream maker and it turned out delicious too. Marvellous if served just with small sponge fingers or macaroons, but absolutely sensational with:

Flambéd apples

5 small eating apples
1 tablespoon butter
2 heaped tablespoons icing
  sugar

1 small wineglass white wine
2 generous liqueur glasses
  Calvados

Peel, core and halve the apples. Melt the butter in a shallow, flameproof dish, add the apples and the wine. Leave to simmer gently until the apples are cooked but not mushy, then turn up the heat for the syrup from the apples to thicken and lightly caramelize. Gently warm the Calvados, pour over the apples and set alight. Serve at once, accompanied by the ice-cold chestnut mousse.

Rich chocolate icecream

5 oz (140g) bitter chocolate   5 oz (140g) icing sugar
¾ pint (425ml) milk   1 teaspoon vanilla sugar
5 egg yolks

Set the refrigerator control at maximum. Grate the chocolate or break it into small pieces. Put the milk into a thick saucepan, add the chocolate and heat very gently until the chocolate has dissolved – do not allow it to come to the boil, and stir it to make sure the chocolate is dissolving and not catching at the bottom of the pan.

Whisk together the egg yolks, icing sugar and vanilla sugar until very light and frothy, and pale yellow in colour. Gradually add the hot milk and chocolate, whisking all the time. Return the mixture to the stove in a double boiler and stir until it has thickened. (You can return the pan to the stove over direct heat, but in that case the heat has to be very low indeed and the mixture will want extra attention, otherwise it will curdle.) Remove from the heat, stir until cool – this can be accelerated by plunging the saucepan into a bowl of crushed ice.

Pour the cold mixture into the icecube tray, having removed the partitions. Cover with foil and put it into the freezing compartment of the refrigerator. Stir during the freezing or, better still, break up the mixture and whisk it – or put it through the food processor – then return it to complete freezing.

If you have an icecream machine, simply put the cold chocolate mixture into the tin provided, close the lid and then put the machine into the freezing compartment of the refrigerator and switch on the machine. It will do the rest – and stop when the icecream has reached the right consistency.

Caramel icecream

4 oz (110g) caster sugar
½ pint (350ml) milk or single
 cream

1 teaspoon vanilla sugar
2 egg yolks
1 egg

Put the caster sugar into a thick saucepan, add just enough water to prevent it from burning, and let it melt over a low flame. Stir until the sugar has dissolved, then turn up the heat and leave to cook without stirring until the sugar has turned golden brown.

Meanwhile – in a separate pan – heat all but two tablespoons of the milk or cream with the vanilla sugar. As soon as the sugar has turned golden brown add the warmed milk and leave over a low flame until the caramel has dissolved completely.

Whisk together the egg yolks and the whole egg with the two tablespoons of milk or cream which have been set aside. Slowly pour the caramel milk on to the egg mixture, whisking all the time. Return to the stove in a double boiler and cook gently until the mixture has thickened and will cover the back of a spoon. Remove from the fire and leave to cool, stirring from time to time.

Set the refrigerator control at maximum. Put the caramel cream into the icecream maker, set it in the freezing compartment of the refrigerator and switch on – the machine will do the rest.

If you have not got an icecream maker, simply freeze the mixture in the icecube tray, having removed the partitions. Tip it into a bowl after it has frozen, whisk, and return the mixture to the freezing tray. Repeat breaking-up and whisking once more for a smooth finish.

Peach sorbet

1 lb (450g) ripe peaches,
  skinned and stoned
¾ pint (425ml) water
12 oz (340g) granulated
  sugar

juice of ½ lemon
dash of peach brandy

Set the refrigerator control at maximum. Dissolve the sugar in the water, bring to the boil and cook for 4–5 minutes. Leave to cool.

Purée the peaches – either in a liquidizer or in a food processor or, failing that, rub them through a sieve. If using a food processor or liquidizer, add the cooled sugar solution while processing. If the fruit has been rubbed through a sieve, stir in the sugar solution. Add lemon juice and peach brandy. Pour the mixture into the icecube tray – or trays – having first removed the partitions, and allow to freeze. Tip the mixture into a bowl and whisk until smooth and frothy (you can also use a food processor for this). Return the mixture to the freezing compartment and repeat the breaking-up and whisking procedure once more.

If you have an icecream-making machine, just tip the purée, sugar solution, lemon juice and peach brandy into the receptacle provided, clamp on the lid and put the machine into the freezing compartment of the refrigerator and switch on – the machine will do the rest.

Melon sorbet

11 oz (300g) ripe honeydew
   melon, weighed after
   peeling
2 fl oz (50ml) gin

2 fl oz (50ml) water
1½–2 oz (40–50g) icing
   sugar, depending on
   sweetness of melon

Set the refrigerator control at maximum. Sprinkle the melon with sugar, add water and gin, and purée everything in a blender or food processor, or push through a sieve.

Proceed as for peach sorbet.

Redcurrant water ice

1 lb (450g) redcurrants
juice of ½ lemon

1 teaspoon vanilla sugar
sugar syrup (see page 192)

Wash the redcurrants and put them through the blender – stems and all. You will have to fish out the stems from the blender blades, but it is worth the trouble since much of the redcurrant flavour is contained in the stems. Now sieve the resulting pulp which in turn will result in a rather liquid purée. Measure it, add the same quantity of sugar syrup, the lemon juice and the vanilla sugar. Chill well. If you have an icecream machine, simply put the mixture into the machine, close the lid and put it into the freezing compartment of the refrigerator, having previously turned it to maximum, and let the machine do the work. If you have not got an icecream machine, put the mixture into the freezing tray, having removed the partitions, cover it with foil and set it to freeze.

When the mixture is half-frozen, tip it into a bowl, whisk well with a rotary whisk and return the mixture to the refrigerator. Repeat this procedure once more for a really smooth ice. (Half a stiffly beaten egg white can be incorporated into the mixture after the second 'breaking up' – it will make for an even lighter texture.)

Index

Index

Index